ACTIVATE YOUR
BEAST MODE

ABHIJIT KOLAS
POOJA NAIK

BLUEROSE PUBLISHERS
India | U.K.

Copyright © Abhijit Kolas & Pooja Naik 2024

All rights reserved by author. No part of this publication may be reproduced, stored in a retrieval system or transmitted in any form or by any means, electronic, mechanical, photocopying, recording or otherwise, without the prior permission of the author. Although every precaution has been taken to verify the accuracy of the information contained herein, the publisher assume no responsibility for any errors or omissions. No liability is assumed for damages that may result from the use of information contained within.

BlueRose Publishers takes no responsibility for any damages, losses, or liabilities that may arise from the use or misuse of the information, products, or services provided in this publication.

For permissions requests or inquiries regarding this publication, please contact:

BLUEROSE PUBLISHERS
www.BlueRoseONE.com
info@bluerosepublishers.com
+91 8882 898 898
+4407342408967

ISBN: 978-93-6452-781-1

Cover design: Tahira
Typesetting: Tanya Raj Upadhyay

First Edition: July 2024

Navarasa
Express yourself

Foreword

Activate Your Beast Mode takes you on a transformative journey through the maze of challenges and triumphs that define the path to peak performance. This book delves into the essence of harnessing your full potential across various aspects of life, emphasizing mastery over everyday tasks with efficiency, grace, and equanimity, while transcending the constraints of time and resources.

The core message is that success isn't about the quantity of time but how we manage and utilize each moment. Through insightful narratives and numerous actionable tips, the book reveals how even the busiest individuals can carve out time for themselves, balance their responsibilities, and maintain harmony even in adversity.

This integrated approach guides you through strategies to conquer procrastination, elevate your strengths, and re-define your limits, focusing on conditioning both mind and body. Each chapter, from "See the Big Picture" to "Sleep Peacefully", offers a roadmap for bringing excitement and enjoyment to both personal and professional life.

Activate Your Beast Mode is more than a guide; it is a powerful catalyst for personal transformation and achieving true peak performance. It will be your companion in activating not just your beast mode, but your best mode.

Dr. Vijay Bhatkar

Motivation

Having been through similar experiences multiple times, repeatedly encountering situations where commitments must be honored across various facets of life—be it professional success, academic achievement, or sustaining relationships—I've often pondered: I'm not alone in this exciting journey. Millions of others navigate similar challenges. It's not about doing something exceptional; rather, it's about completing routine tasks with limited time and resources. I believe everyone encounters such tight spots. This book aims to explore these situations from diverse perspectives, addressing challenges and triumphing over them convincingly.

Let me give you an example. Every person on earth is granted exactly 24 hours in a day. There are no exceptions, yet we see some "gifted" people who can find time to party after work, who get to spend quality time with family, who never look stressed, who revere their hobbies while managing busy schedules, while there are a plenty who just slog and forego the peace of darkness. Let's try changing perspectives and zooming the available time in and out. A simple math tells us that 24 hours equals 1440 minutes, or 86400 seconds. Let's look at different perspectives. When you look at a time span in terms of hours, you tend to spend more. So, if you say you want to take a quick power nap of half an hour, think over it again; you end up spending 15 minutes more than if you say you want to take a quick power nap of fifteen minutes! A power nap is just a peaceful state of mind where you let your brain relax from all the mental noise and stress and get back to work with refreshed energy levels.

Start applying this in your routine and you will suddenly find that you have plenty of excess time that you can utilize in interesting ways. If your boss asks you how much time do need to complete a certain piece of work, start thinking right away in terms of minutes rather than days and hours. Believe me, you're in for a massive breakthrough.

This book is all about making several such simple and interesting tweaks in a typical routine in the quest of achieving peak performance. The tweaks mentioned in this book are a result of experimenting and experiencing with myself, my colleagues and friends, and there is a fair chance that these techniques will work for you too.

I urge you to keep this book as your companion on your office desk, in your travel bag and your vacation kit. The book is not organized in any sequence, the compelling reason being you open any page, and you'll find something that you can correlate with your life and apply right away for great results.

How to read this book

The book is written in a simple language, with minimal to no use of difficult or exotic words. It is meant to be easily understood by everyone right from an intern to a seasoned top manager. Each chapter is purposely short and spans just one to two pages.

This book mainly seeks to give some insights into common work-related challenges and how to deal with them in practical ways. By breaking the chapters down into small units, the book encourages readers to interact with every paragraph, read it slowly, relate with own experiences and go through them again.

The title of each chapter is a self-explanatory action item. Hence, read it carefully, a couple of times, before jumping down to the text. Each chapter contains some tips on how you can go about achieving the action item. The given tips are not exhaustive and are provided just as indicative starters to ignite further thought process on those lines.

Don't be in a hurry to finish off the book in one go! Read just one chapter a day. Read it chapter carefully, several times.
Keep a pen and paper handy to take down notes from your own experience if you find some similarity. Follow the checklist and note down your own resolutions for achieving the action items.

Performance Catalysts

1. See the big picture 1
2. Build a story 5
3. Gift yourself three hours 8
4. Find yourself in the corner 12
5. Learn and practice multitasking 15
6. Plan your project 19
7. Live your project 22
8. Have milestones with tangible outcomes ... 25
9. Stay healthy 28
10. Communicate effectively 31
11. Learn the art of typing 36
12. Make a template for mechanical tasks ... 39
13. Maintain the arrogance you deserve ... 43
14. Keep teams engaged 47
15. Motivate yourself 51
16. Be in control of your project 55
17. Someone must do the actual work, you be the one ... 58
18. Save 90 minutes a day with smart work ... 61
19. Understand that stress is just a state of mind ... 65
20. Nurture a hobby 69
21. Identify your leadership spot 73
22. Do not hesitate to experiment 77
23. Commit to your commitment 81
24. Maintain a comfortable posture 84
25. Inform in advance 87
26. Spring a surprise 90
27. Learn the art of selective listening .. 94
28. Stay ahead in your field 99
29. Learn the art of unlearning 103
30. Learn reporting craftsmanship 108
31. What's holding you back? 112
32. Learn the art of detachment 116
33. Enter the uncharted waters 120
34. Have patience 123

35.	Give examples that connect	127
36.	Learn the art of expectation management	131
37.	Don't miss that thing	134
38.	Begin where the strongest ends	137
39.	Identify your turning point	140
40.	There is always a room to accommodate	144
41.	Treat everything as primary activity	148
42.	Strive for longevity	151
43.	Learn the art of compartmentalizing	154
44.	Get everyone on a common page	158
45.	Find your "It all began with…" moment	162
46.	Be uncomfortable	165
47.	Find yourself in wondrous amazement	169
48.	Your best is yet to come	173
49.	Pour in your head, heart and soul	176
50.	Sleep peacefully	179

1

See the big picture

Keywords, buzzwords, jargons, and opinions – You often get these in abundance at the start of a project, especially in a new domain or technology, leading to a familiar situation, which is popularly known as "chaos". Ponder over it for a minute, and I'm sure you'll recall yourself caught in a similar condition at some point. As a special characteristic of this chaotic scenario, you often find everyone running in every direction, to prove a point, make a mark, and get the first advantage.

But wait! You don't have to join that race, you can stand out and still out stand. Understand the gist of the concept, put together a high-level picture, and you will feel in control already. Irrespective of the domain, technology, or size, the big picture strategy helps understand all aspects of the project, the components, their interconnections, and you get a clear idea to set it up in a proper workflow. Once you have mapped all these components, you can confidently move forward in executing the project with total control.

Here's a checklist to visualize the big picture and take the leadership position.

✔ Avoid getting overwhelmed. It's natural to panic when faced with a problem, especially when it comes with extraneous details. Focus on filtering out the noise to identify the core issue and build your solution around the focal point.

✔ Listen to your customer carefully; put in serious effort to read between the lines. Pay close attention and strive to understand the underlying issues behind a customer's request. Often, new requirements grow from an unpleasant experience, so their narrative may be emotionally charged. Hence, it is important to "discover" the true need hidden beneath their expressed concerns.

✔ Decompose the problem. Suppose you are posed with a problem statement as, "I want to build an ERP that will consist of all the modules that will cater to all our departments, be mobile responsive, handle third party integrations, has data analytics, and comply with relevant industry standards such as GDPR, HIPAA, or SOX". Now, that's a lot of keywords. Break it down into smaller components. See what's within your domain, rest you can filter out and keep limited only to the interface level.

✔ Filter all the noise. Retain only what is relevant for the problem in question. Take a pen and paper and write down those components, preferably in the form of block diagram. Something scribbled visually will help in grasping the overall structure and focusing only on essential elements.

✔ Assemble all your knowledge and experience. Use your expertise to develop a high-level concept, which will help you gain a sense of control over the problem.

✔ Prepare contingency plans. Start working on Plan B and consider the possibility of having a Plan C to ensure you are prepared for any eventualities.

The big picture is primarily for yourself, to make you feel comfortable. Scribble it on a piece of paper, build a relationship with your work, carry it with you everywhere, keep looking at it again and again to validate, refine and let your sub-conscious mind do the detailing in the background.

You can apply the big picture technique to any kind of activity, irrespective of size, domain, or complexity. Remember, when you have your eyes on the outcome, you get solutions to interim problems almost magically.

"Chase the big picture; hurdles will then only seem to be minor hiccups; others might find those as major blockades."

2

Build a story

Imagine a big budget movie with a glaring star cast, excellent cinematography, mesmerizing music, breathtaking action, lively direction, and yet that falls flat on the box office. You may have come across several such movies, the simple reason being that of a missing storyline that is meaningful, compelling, and engaging. On the other hand, you would find plenty of movies from the golden era that were technologically bereft, low budget, simple setup, yet massively successful; the reason - a storyline that one could easily relate to and get connected with it.

Your routine work is no different. Frame it in a monotonous template, limit yourself by the boundaries of this template, wait for the boring feeling to take over, and find yourself wandering in search of "something new". A better approach is to get back to the big picture, identify the sweet spot which you can consider as the anchor of your project, build a story around it and relish the smallest of achievements in that storyline.

The project can be anything, absolutely any set of activities you can think of in achieving any objective, irrespective of size. Try applying this technique in activities such as working with disgruntled teams, designing home or office interior, communicating with an annoyed customer, preparing a delicious recipe, taking your child to a dentist, tackling an illness, creating a concept document, preparing a presentation; the possibilities are limitless.

Here's how you can build a story:

- Start with a theme that will define the orientation of your activities. Choose a word that describes the theme, such as, speed, excellence, happiness, automation, satisfaction, or any other you feel relevant.

- Start living the theme, by convincing yourself through affirmations such as, "My project will be characterized by speed, everything I do in this project will be done at 2x speed"; "I want to reduce my work by automating everything that I see to be repeating more than thrice"; "I'll make my daughter's visit to the dentist an experience that she'll enjoy".

✔ Identify all the actors that will participate in your story, do not limit to just humans. Remember that you are the lead actor!

✔ Explore ways that you can associate the theme with your actors. Assuming your theme is energy, start thinking of ways you can bring out energy in everything that comes your way during your project, and you being the lead actor, strive to be energetic yourself.

✔ Find all those small events in your project where you think you can apply the theme.

✔ Connect all events in a consistent flow that culminates into your end objective.

"Your own little experiences are a wonderful story in the making. Stay conscious, live the experience, learn from it, and you'll have a great story to tell."

3

Gift yourself three hours

Imagine someone with an empty bank account, and suddenly, a million bucks appear in that account. Wow, that's big money. One could book a vehicle, take up all the long overdue house repairs, get nice clothes, invest for better returns, or do anything else that was lying idle in the wish list just for want of that "extra" funds.

Now, imagine yourself with a long wish list of to-dos, but couldn't take up any of those, just because you're running short of time. You are not alone, most of us go through this impasse. There are so many things that we plan but remain just a plan only for want of time. A typical workday squeezes out all of your time, and you are left in search of that "free" time on some other day, which ironically, doesn't "appear".

Well, you can easily (of course, with some initial conflict between your logical and emotional mind) gift yourself three hours a day, all for yourself to focus on all that you always wanted to do. Remember the adage, "Early to bed, early to rise, makes a man healthy, wealthy and wise"? It's time to put it back into action. Begin your day at 4 am, and you will suddenly find yourself amidst 3 - 4 serene hours when you have your mind and brain fresh and relaxed.

Although I prefer 4 am, you may find peace at night. The point is you must put in that extra effort for getting those extra hours yet taking the required minimum sleep of 6 hours.

Do you wake up at 8? Do you want to start early to get an additional three hours? Here's how you can start.

✔ Find a reason; get obsessed with a purpose; keep thinking about it; get driven by it. It could be any reason – a hobby idea, learning a musical instrument, reading a book, exploring technology, excelling at a subject topic, creating a concept, or writing a book like I am doing.

✔ Make a firm resolve to get up early tomorrow with this obsession in mind. Don't wait for an auspicious day to make this new beginning!

✔ Keep telling yourself that you are going to sleep an hour earlier than your daily routine; plan your day accordingly.

✔ Set an alarm, just one alarm. Don't fall into the trap of setting up a second alarm in case you fall asleep after snoozing. That's the comfort zone you must get out of!

✔ The fun begins when you hear the alarm, and you lose the opportunity in the "settlement" between your logical mind (LM) and emotional mind (EM). The scene goes like this…

Alarm rings…

EM: I had a disturbed sleep last night.
(you may have your own reasons, and there are plenty of them);
Let me sleep for another 10 minutes.
and you snooze it... **ZZZ**

LM: Alright, but only 10 minutes.

EM: Just 10 minutes, it's a promise.

LM: Go ahead.

A few minutes later…ZZZZZZZZZZ

EM: Oh no, it's 7:30

LM: What's the point of getting up now? You have already missed the chance, better sleep today, and start fresh tomorrow.

EM: You're right.

This goes on for a few days, until you convince yourself, getting up in the wee hours isn't your style, and you prefer to remain in your routine comfort zone.

So, try not to listen to your logical mind or emotional mind. Just choose to rise. You have the capacity; you have done this several times in the past. Remember, when you had to catch up that early morning flight, or to travel with your boss early in the morning, or for the maintenance activity in the off-peak hours?

"Do not buy time, when you already have aplenty"

4
Find yourself in the corner

Dejected; depressed; defeated; demotivated; demoralized; clueless; helpless; cornered. Did you ever get this kind of feeling? Well, everyone does, at some point or the other, for reasons such as personal, professional, academic, relationships and more. Getting in such a situation and realizing that you are there is what I call finding yourself in the corner. "Realizing" that you are in the corner is very important, because this means you are aware and can activate the extra gear to come out in winning ways.

If you fail to realize that you are helpless, then it is safe to assume that you are not in control, rather circumstances are controlling you. When your life is not in your control, you try to find ways of running away from the situation, the recent favorites being to resign, switch, divorce, or suicide. Although these are the easy runaways, choose to go against these, and against suicide at every cost.

So, the key is to be mindful of the fact that you are helpless. The exciting journey begins when you know that you are starved, as "starvation is the mother of all creativity". Look back at the history of all inventions, and you'll realize that there was some kind of frustration, starvation, that led to the invention of what we use today as necessity.

We often prioritize saving even during prosperity as it reflects a thoughtful approach to finances. By building a security nest we are prepared for unexpected events, future goals, and unforeseen fluctuations. On similar lines, it is important to preserve all the small units of knowledge that you gain – could be a simple formula, a shortcut, a library, a layout, or anything else. It is not necessary to be a master in everything, but it is important to be aware that something exists and can be handy as a secret weapon to free yourself from the corner.

Here's how you can break out from the corner:

- See the big picture, again.

- Take a pause, assess the situation, and decide to go against the flow.

- Identify all those unfavorable components that constitute the situation.

- Divide and conquer is the mantra. Break down the components (could be people, technology, understanding or anything else), into attainable milestones.

- Prepare an actionable checklist on a piece of paper.

- Allocate a slice of your time to each such item in the checklist.

- Depart from the way you were approaching this problem so far; think out of the box; think of alternative ways of handling it.

- Invoke all the knowledge you have gained, and it will rescue you from hopeless situations.

- Put a checkmark on achieving every single item in your list, and remember to celebrate the success, with yourself, in your own mind. Every small bit of success sums up your confidence and works wonders for self-motivation.

Apply this in your work, relationships, studies, and you'll find great versions of yourself that you never knew, always existed within you.

"If you withstand the pressure after getting pushed in the corner, then the result is invariably going to be a great success."

5
Learn and practice multitasking

If you have witnessed the evolution of computing processors, you would easily relate how the processors have evolved from humble beginnings of single tasking into dual, quad, octa and an ever-growing number of cores, to accommodate the increased computing demands.

Can humans multitask? Well, if you Google, you'd probably find contrasting views. However, if you "realize" to have "found yourself in the corner" you have no option but to utilize your time optimally. Let's call this outcome a result of efficient working, or the process, multitasking.

So, how exactly can you multitask? Let's go back to see how the computer works to find our answer. Let's say you are editing a document. You will notice that you can type in only one active window at a time. However, the computer does not remain idle, it performs its own tasks, by listening to network and system events, and processing maintenance activities. For example, while typing you might also be listening to your favorite music, printing a document, and downloading a video, and the computer is busy scanning for viruses. Sounds good?

Let's try to put this in context and build an analogy to find easily achievable avenues for multitasking.

✔ Most important, keep your eyes and ears open, but actively interact with only one activity to remain focused and give justice to the task at hand.

✔ Distinguish between mental and mechanical tasks. Make a conscious effort to make sure your brain is not involved in any mechanical activities.

✔ Typing is a must-have skill, learn it, master it. Efficient typing with eyes only on the screen will reduce it to a pure mechanical activity, helping your mind and brain to think of ideas, solutions, and next steps in parallel rather than keeping your eyes busy shuttling between the keyboard and monitor. Imagine the efficiency gained in thinking about the next part of the logic while you simply key in the already formulated logic, mechanically!

✔ Sleep over problems and you'll get ideas, solutions, and visualizations "automagically". That's the power of the subconscious mind, where you don't actively engage, but your brain does all the computing while you sleep peacefully.

Suppose you are given the task of oscillating several pendulums continuously. You'd obviously not keep pushing them on every single cycle. You'd probably push it once and let it slow down a bit until it needs a further push. Meanwhile you get sufficient time to cycle through the rest, and you'll not even realize that you have hundreds of pendulums oscillating simultaneously. That's smart work! Optimize this further with innovative techniques and you'd be spending even less energy and yet getting the same work done with even more efficiency.

Take a pause and read this once again, try to visualize it this time.

Let's put this into practice. Here's a simple technique on the same principle, to keep waking up your brain for things you often put in the background, and eventually forget or lose the thought process due to prolonged dormancy.

✔ Make a list of all the mental work that circumstances have been forced on you to do in parallel.

✔ Don't keep this list as bullet points on a single page, for the simple reason that whenever you go through an organized list, the flow is top to bottom most of the time, and when that happens, you'll find yourself stuck up right at the top.

- Make a list of all the mental work that circumstances have forced you to do in parallel.

- Don't keep this list as bullet points on a single page, for the simple reason that whenever you go through an organized list, the flow is top to bottom most of the time, and when that happens, you'll find yourself stuck up right at the top.

- Scatter your points in the form of 'Post-It' notes which you wouldn't lose but would see when you take your eyes off the current task in hand.

- Don't fall into the pattern trap, otherwise all your tasks will look the same as boring text. The mind needs disruption to get distracted. Hence try to list your parallel tasks in visually creative ways; keep tinkering with the items every now and then. For example, you can associate a task with a smiley drawn on paper - keep enhancing it with every small progress in the task.

- Keep several browser tabs open, with each tab having something related to your parallel work-in-progress. This will help randomly remind you and just as the pendulum oscillates, give your mind and brain the much-needed push to reinitiate background processing.

I'm sure you will get even better ideas if you explore your creativity to keep your mind occupied, yet not stressed. Our brain has all the capacity to handle several tasks in parallel, and it is already doing so, but the mind gets indulged in random thoughts which means potential wastage of energy. Make a conscious attempt to channelize your mind towards tasks to make your brain wake up to those tasks in some of the ways mentioned above.

6

Plan your project

Have you seen videos of tigers preparing themselves before a grand hunt? It's amazing how they carefully watch their prey, the surroundings, have a Plan-B ready, follow it up with great execution, and almost always end up with a successful hunt unless the prey is another master at execution of its own escape plan! Tigers use the same strategy for hunting, irrespective of whether they are hunting a swift deer, an aggressive wild boar, or smaller prey like a frog.

What do we learn from this? Just like tigers, who meticulously plan every step of their hunt, successful project planning involves a series of thoughtful steps that ensure your goals are met and your efforts are optimized.

What is a project in the context of integrated approach? Well, it is anything that needs to be completed in a set amount of time. It could be a simple assignment, a research paper, mastering a sport or technique, learning a musical instrument, or anything else that you can think of.

You don't have to be a certified project manager; you just need to understand the scope and the technicalities. A project manager can define the larger project, however, as an engineer or a developer, it is in your interest to treat the activities allocated to you as your mini projects. Once you break down your larger project into smaller projects or activities, and plan each of them with enough detailing and follow up with execution as planned, eventually all these work in tandem towards success of your larger project.

I wish to share my experience on how planning a project meticulously and executing it with aplomb can lead to great success. I had yearned for a long time to venture into martial arts. But as they say, intent without action is just as worthless as it can be! I ended up wasting at least ten years just maintaining the intent without action. One fine day, I finally made up my mind and jumped into the journey of attaining Black Belt and swore to do that before turning 50. At the age of 48, this was indeed constrained by time, and I knew with most certainty that I had to put in extra effort into the building blocks of speed, stamina, strength, stability, and flexibility. So, these were the sporting techniques I wanted to master, and thus became my mini projects, each further broken down into focused activities. With no option than to activate beast mode, I planned my project, executed the activities, and by the time of publishing this book, I'm 50 and already a 2nd Dan Black Belt!

Here's a checklist on how you can go about planning your tasks:

- First, know your project.
- Do research on what goes into achieving your objectives.
- Break down your project into achievable tasks.
- Set clear objectives for each of the tasks.
- Plan in detail.
- Resolve to execute with passion and precision.

Sometimes we are so used to our routine that we take planning for granted, and this can bump us into unforeseen challenges. Planning is extremely important, be it driving a complete project, writing a piece of code, or pursuing a hobby idea. Although we see project managers as the ones responsible for planning, it is not completely true. While project managers own the responsibility of the complete project, the task assigned to you is a mini project, that must be planned and executed at the granular level.

Remember, strategic execution of a well-thought-out plan is the key to success. Just like the tiger, live your project with intent, focus, and the agility to adjust with changing circumstances.

7

Live your project

Passion and perseverance are important factors that play a crucial role in the success of any project. How do you infuse passion into your projects? Well, it comes automatically when you start living through your project, making key aspects of the project an integral part of your routine. The way marathoners approach their run is a great lesson in living the projects passionately and with perseverance. They start determined to cross the finish line, and in the process, they overcome fatigue, manage their pace, and adjust to changing terrain. Similarly, you must pour passion into your project and persevere through the challenges. It's all about putting your heart and soul into each task with enthusiasm and not just floating through the project as it moves on.

When you start living your project, you automatically start thinking about all the intricacies in the background, and that is essentially the key to successful planning. It will then come instinctively, that you'll keep on thinking about all those possibilities that can make or break your project. Once you immerse yourself into the details, you will automatically find yourself going beyond the routine to-do list, delving into the project's core, understanding its purpose, impact, and potential challenges. It is at this point that you no longer need anyone else to motivate you, as you are self-motivated at that time.

Imagination plays an important role in helping the cause of living our project. It is like an additive that powers our journey through a project. It helps us anticipate potential obstacles, and it is the same imagination that can present creative ideas. When we switch on the imagination mode, we can envision the future possibilities to make it easy to adapt to changing circumstances.

If you aren't living your project yet, here's a checklist to get started.

- ✔ Use pen and paper to sketch your ideas. Write down key notes for a clear plan to tackle your project.

✔ Imagine you've finished your project successfully. Think of reaching your goals to stay motivated and guiding your work to make that dream real.

✔ It is a good idea to question "what if" and doubt all assumptions to see things in different perspectives. This lets you catch possible issues that could come up and tweak your strategies.

✔ Thinking ahead about potential problems prepares you for them. Once you are aware of these problems, you can work out alternative ways to overcome them.

✔ Your approach may not hold good in the changing circumstances. You must remain agile to tweak and adapt new approaches to the latest changes, staying swift and prepared throughout the project.

✔ Keep your thoughts about the project continue to tick across the clock.

Authoring this book is a deeply personal project, reflecting my experiences over the past 25 years. It all began with creating the "Table of Contents," which established the framework for the book. Thereafter I just continued living the project every day. How? Each chapter addresses a challenge we face daily - be it with people, technology, grievances, and more. I mapped each of these challenges to a chapter, narrating solutions that were either already documented or emerged through the writing process. Believe me, you really must live your project to truly immerse yourself into it!

8

Have milestones with tangible outcomes

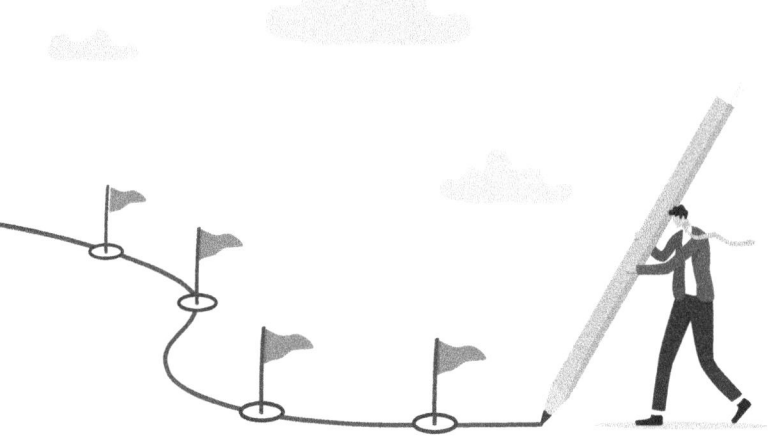

You often assess situations as you perceive them to be, which may be real or may be far from it. It is just your viewpoint that is based on expectations, experiences, and circumstances. In either of these cases your perception is an important driver for the next actions, and as it is popularly said, perceptions are real because the consequences are real.

Hence, build your perceptions by taking a neutral view, by empathizing with the other actors, understanding their point of view, assumptions, constraints, and desired outcomes. Chances of perceptions to be real are much higher if they are based on such foundations.

"The conflict is never between you and them; it is always between you and your perceptions."

The above was just to set the context right, because sometimes you are the assessor, while most of the time you are the one being assessed by several assessors, which often includes yourself, well unknowingly!

So, we have handled the first part where you are the assessor. It is simple and straightforward (if you keep an open mind) because you are in control and define what, how and why and build your perception.

What happens when you are being assessed? It's simple. Pretend to be the assessor, and you'll immediately know what is required to make others see what you want them to see. When I say "assess", I do not mean a formal assessment, it is rather what you endure almost every day at work or at home.

Suppose you are working on a project that requires a lot of study, research, experimentation, thought, and the outcome, uncertain. You may be doing some intense work in the background, but for the stakeholders such as your colleagues, superiors, and clients, it might be a "black box". This is the anxious period where perceptions start taking shape, and this is the time you must control what you want others to see.

- Remember the mantra "Seeing is believing", hence "showing is instilling that belief".

- An animation looks dynamic and happening than a still picture. Apply the same principle and define smaller milestones that will have something visible to give your stakeholders the feel that the project is moving.

- Define and convey the assumptions and limitations of each milestone and your refinement plan, also with tangible outcome. Doing this upfront will help perceive how you want it to be perceived.

- Keep your stakeholders informed of all that you think would add up to the "Wow!" factor, including anticipated delays and expected problems, besides the positive aspects.

- Having smaller and tangible milestones also helps in timely course correction rather than discovering something undesired later.

- More than anyone else, it is important that you celebrate your milestones and keep yourself going.

By managing perceptions through strategies like these, you can ensure a clearer, more positive understanding of your efforts and progress, ultimately leading to better outcomes.

9
Stay healthy

Do you feel vibrant, energetic, resilient every morning, and balanced, harmonious and peaceful while you go to bed? Chances are probably not, as we are living in the age of extended work hours, pressure, and stress. The good news is, everyone can, with a dedicated effort towards health and well-being. Being healthy isn't just a hope; it's a choice we make by acting on it. It's about creating a good way of living, choosing wisely, and taking care of our whole self.

Health is indeed wealth, and nurturing this wealth demands intentional effort. As a part of your work routine, there will be physical and mental stress for reasons beyond your control. You must beat the stress that life throws at you by channeling your energy into a sport or physical activity. Craft a new world for you, far from daily dullness, by adding in fun, happiness, and novelty to your every single day. Stay in good health to feel calm, knowing that a clear mind is vital for feeling great all over.

Challenge yourself to keep a distance from medicines by adopting preventive healthcare practices. Develop a strong aversion to hospitalization by choosing a lifestyle that minimizes the likelihood of medical emergencies. Choose what you eat and how much you eat, understanding that your dietary choices play a crucial role in shaping your health.

Your life is like a play area, and you're the one testing things out. Take on this journey with a helpful way of thinking, trying out good changes that make your health better. Just like knowing you're stuck is key to getting past troubles, keeping an eye on your health lets you pick paths that make your life full and well.

Here's how you can stay healthy:

- Recognize that health is your true wealth.
- Make a dedicated effort towards staying healthy.
- Get into a sport or some intense physical activity.
- Subscribe to a yoga class and make it a point to not miss it.
- Keenly observe and caress yourself.
- Listen to your body, try to interpret what it's trying to say.
- Feel and celebrate muscle pain after a workout. It's an indication that your body got "that missing stretch".
- Give your mind and brain a few minutes off with quality power naps.
- Introduce variety and joy to create a different world for yourself.
- If at all you fall sick, take all the sympathy you get, but with a pinch of salt.
- Be wary of addictions, they can take control over you without your knowledge.

"Focus on your health, and you'll discover versions of yourself that you never knew existed—healthy, vibrant, and thriving."

10
Communicate effectively

We are talking about achieving peak performance using an integrated approach, which includes tweaking a multitude of factors in a typical routine. There's no way that effective communication can stay out of this list, for it is the one thing that can make or break, engage or disengage, and hence has a direct bearing on your project. While effective communication demands a lot of practice and application, here are some simple techniques that you can apply in your routine, to enhance your performance as well as help others positively perceive your performance.

- Your name is the most important word for you, and this applies to any other person as well. Never misspell anyone's name, as it depicts disrespect and hurts the reader.

- Write as if everything is poetry, whether prose or poem; you'll automatically get ideas for interesting words and forming sentences logically.

- Respect is always mutual; you get it only when you give. Non-committal communication amounts to disrespect and that works dangerously at the subconscious level.

- Take a deep breath, become neutral and then hold the pen. Your mind will be pure and thoughts clear, and that will automatically show in your writing.

- Good writing is never accidental. You should profile the readers and customize and personalize. Remember that one shoe doesn't fit all.

- Consider that the first paragraph is your last opportunity to make the first impression. Hence, compose your opening statement to grab maximum positive attention and generate sufficient curiosity to keep the reader hooked until the end.

- Even something that is scribbled by a two-year-old is appreciated. Thus, understand that the context is important, not the use of rare or amusing words.

- Write emails with sufficient evidence to support your point of view. Doing this will reduce a lot of to-and-fro communication and will help you save time.

- Some words sound alike but have different meanings altogether. Use these words after careful consideration.

- Remember to capitalize the first letter of all proper nouns.

- Use either US or UK convention, don't mix both in a single document.

- There are only a few people who are blessed with spontaneous writing or oratory skills; others require meticulous planning.

- Your words are valued when you yourself value them. Hence, a commitment once made, must be fulfilled, whatever it takes. Every commitment, irrespective of size, impact or purpose is equally important.

- Write intelligently. Leave a loophole only if you see something coming back to you. For example, open ended statements such as "Please address on priority" can be easily exploited. Make intelligent use of such statements, both as a reader and composer.

- Spice up your letter occasionally by using appropriate idioms. For example, you should "leave no stone unturned" in this quest for better writing.

- "I" symbolizes me, my ego, my story, and less of you. Use it carefully, especially when writing on behalf of a team or company.

- Identify the sweet spot of the context in question and revolve your story around it to have the perfect appeal.

- Presentation plays a key role in anything you do, whether cooking or writing. Hence factors such as use of good fonts, colors, alignment, spacing, and pictures are very important.

- While you are free to take the reader through past, present and future, make sure that you maintain grammatically correct tenses in your writing.

- One spelling mistake equals one sin, one abuse and one crime. Can you afford any of these? Just think on these lines and you will be perfect.

- Do not rush to click the send button when writing sensitive emails. Write, think, revise, contemplate, revise, and then send. Make use of the Save Draft facility.

- Keep your lines short and simple, as you are writing not to demonstrate your writing ability, but to convey what you intend to…correctly.

- Make sure that your sentence follows the same thought process as the punctuation marks.

- Occasionally use the alliteration style of writing for greater emphasis, such as 3 C's, 3 D's, 3 E's. For example, you could write "down, disturbed and distressed" to indicate a feeling of being let down, or "clear, concise, correct" to indicate guidelines for communication.

✔ Think from your heart, moderate with your mind, and write with your brain. Use AI writing tools such as ChatGPT sparingly. Although these tools can write beautifully, they may not express the same feelings that you would in your original style.

✔ Don't confront. Accept, if it is your mistake.

✔ When you receive a job offer, email platforms such as Gmail give you quick response buttons such as "I accept the offer", saving you some time. But wait! This is your first formal interaction with your employer. This first interaction might as well act as the last opportunity to make the first impression. Take a moment to thank your employer by composing your own acceptance of the job offer.

11
Learn the art of typing

Let's picture a construction site bustling with activity. While hundreds of workers carry out labor-intensive tasks, a select group of skilled engineers oversee the technical intricacies. The workers don't have to get into the thinking process, they must just implement to perfection the skill they already possess, most of which is mechanical. Now imagine what happens if the handful of skilled engineers also start participating in the laborious work. They will just not be able to do any justice to the mental work that they are supposed to do, because while they might enjoy the laborious work as a stress buster, it will be at a massive cost of productivity.

If your work involves a lot of activity on computer, and you must do a lot of typing, such as writing emails, programs, documenting, or preparing reports, then you must master this skill because it deals with freeing up mental space, allowing you to think clearly and process information more efficiently even while seemingly engaged in another more intensive task.

Typing with fluency and precision unlocks endless opportunities, letting your thoughts flow freely without the constraints of slow or inaccurate typing. Imagine writing code, your mind and eyes constantly switching between the screen and keyboard, frequently hitting backspace to fix mistakes. Wouldn't it be wonderful to focus on logic as your main task, and let that part of your brain which handles physical signals handle the typing work?

Imagine another scenario where you're brimming with ideas, eager to capture them in writing. However, the act of typing itself becomes a bottleneck, hindering the flow of your thoughts. This is where the importance of mastering typing truly makes it prominence felt. When you can effortlessly translate your thoughts into words without conscious effort, it's as if an invisible barrier is lifted, allowing you to think and type simultaneously, focus on creativity, boost productivity, and inch towards peak performance.

If you believe you are a self-taught 2-finger typist that can type at around 45 wpm, I urge you to read the chapter "Learn the art of unlearning", where I have given an example of how you can upgrade yourself from a 2-finger typist to a 9-finger technical typist and achieve great improvement in your speed and accuracy.

Remember, effortless typing is a skill that is often overlooked, but it's a transparent bridge between your mind and your output.

"When fingers dance with fluency across the keyboard, your mind enjoys the freedom to indulge in logic and creativity."

12

Make a template for mechanical tasks

The path to peak performance isn't paved with heroic efforts alone. You must understand that the greatest enemy of efficiency is mundane, repetitive tasks. These are the performance and efficiency bottlenecks that must be tamed as they tend to drain mental energy, steal our focus, and clutter our days. We are talking about those activities which seem insignificant individually but can largely hamper productivity when looked at collectively. What if you could reclaim several hours each week just by streamlining these activities? In turn, you'll be freeing your mind for higher-level thinking and creativity. That's the power of creating templates for mechanical tasks, and I urge you to find such villains in your daily routine, tame them, and utilize those "extra" hours in something productive, creative, that you'll find much more engaging and entertaining.

Templates offer a structured approach to completing tasks with precision and speed. It's akin to creating a library of "Standard Operating Procedures" or "sequences" that can be invoked whenever demanded.

If you are someone into extensive email communication for work, you have likely created a standard email signature to streamline your communication. You probably did this because you wanted a standard way of conveying your regards to the recipient; to avoid spelling "Thnaks" instead of "Thanks", or "Reagards" instead of "Regards"; to avoid mistyping your mobile number; gain overall efficiency, consistency, and accuracy in this mundane but important activity; and save a few minutes!

Here's how you can go about digging out time, that could otherwise be a wasted effort:

- ✔ Recognize the patterns. The first thing to do when creating a template for mechanical tasks is to identify recurring activities in your work. It may be helpful to step back and look at your daily routines for repeated actions. For instance, you will realize that many tasks have a similar set of steps or involve repetitive tasks even in specific programs like Notepad and Excel. Consider a situation where you are supposed to monitor standard emails and "extract" it for further processing, with hundreds of such emails received daily! Would it not be wise then to spare some time and automate the "extraction" and "transformation" a little?

✔ Don't reinvent the wheel. One of the key principles behind creating templates for mechanical tasks is to avoid reinventing the wheel for repetitive activities. Instead of starting from scratch each time, leverage existing templates, or create your own. Pre-made document templates, VBA macros, etc. are a great way to deal with templating.

✔ Formulate keystrokes and mouse moves. This one might seem trivial but plays a significant role of booster in activities that are purely mechanical and involves use of keyboard keys such as the arrow keys, backspace, delete, spacebar, ENTER, Ctrl-C, and Ctrl-V. Repetitive tasks often involve specific keystrokes and mouse movements. Think of your keyboard and mouse as instruments in the orchestra of your productivity. Gain familiarity with the sounds produced by the keyboard and optimize your posture to create comfortable sequences for these actions. This is for those activities that are purely mundane, cannot be automated beyond a limit, and there is no way out but to accept the work that must be done in the same way, yet you must find enjoyment!

✔ Think outside the box. Let's imagine you are an Adobe Photoshop operator tasked with creating some certificates in a standard form, with photo, name and some other details that are going to change. The obvious way especially for beginners and non-programmers is to go about this task by efficient handling of copy/paste. However, the moment you see yourself doing something more than thrice, you must believe that there could be a better, smarter way. Like in this case, you'll have to cross the barriers of your non-programming background and look for ways to automate Photoshop with a bit of scripting! Once you start scouting for such smart solutions, often, you are likely to find a better way out.

So, next time you see yourself doing something repetitive, take a step back and examine if there is a pattern, and try to tame it!

"Your best effort may not be your best as there always exists a better way... Challenge yourself to surpass yourself."

13
Maintain the arrogance you deserve

Arrogance. It's a word that gets thrown around a lot, usually with a negative sentiment. It often pictures individuals giving importance to oneself, the ones that "know it all", the stubborn ones that are averse to ideas or suggestions, the ones whose ego surpasses their achievements, and hence the missing humility.

Arrogance has a healthy side though! If used appropriately, this can be a potent weapon that can propel your performance to new heights. Let's call it the "arrogance you deserve", the one that isn't about blind ego or putting others down. It's about acknowledging your brilliance. Think about it. You have poured your heart, soul, and passion into your work. You have tackled obstacles, worked tirelessly, and emerged as a master in your own right. Only you know the playing field that was offered by the constraints and circumstances. You deserve immense pride in what you've accomplished.

This "arrogance" is not about putting others down; it's about knowing your worth. Let's say you have designed a software system that you consider an achievement, not because it is a technological marvel, but because of the underlying story of your struggle – time constraint, resource crunch, lack of funds, market pressure etc. Despite all this, you've made the system work. Remarkable indeed.

You are the architect of your success. Every challenge that you have overcome, every skill that you have acquired, is written all over your work. Own that. This pride isn't arrogance, it's confidence. It's the quiet understanding that whispers, "I've put in the work, I've put in my best effort and the outcome is the best that was possible in the given context".

Imagine someone who doesn't have knowledge of the depth of what you have been through, strolling in and casually throwing down criticism about your work. It's like offering unsolicited advice on brain surgery to an experienced brain surgeon after watching a YouTube video on "home remedies". Does that sound fair? Absolutely not.

So, how do you carry the confidence of your work on your shoulders, without sounding arrogant? Here's a checklist that will help "channelize your arrogance" and create a perception in the form it deserves:

- Understand that confidence doesn't equal close-mindedness. Welcome respectful dialogue, be open to learning and refining but protect your focus from uninformed noise.

- Listen actively, but don't blindly accept every suggestion. Analyze it through the lens of your experience.

- Although your work speaks for itself, present it in the right frame by documenting your journey. This serves as a tangible reminder of your capabilities, a shield against self-doubt, and a powerful tool when someone questions your work.

- When presenting your work, do so with confidence, supplemented by data, research, and results.

- It's very easy to undermine the effort of someone, as we see only one aspect of the "big picture" that we understand. Hence, keep this in mind when you are in the observing role. By appreciating the role of each individual in the big picture, you'll automatically generate a perception of yourself as one that understands both sides of the fence.

I'll give an example. This book is a summary of my experience, my challenges and my triumphs spread over three decades, and I have written it in a certain way I thought would be right to consume. But, as many people, as many views. Hence, everyone will have a say on various aspects of the book – topics, language, length, size, fonts, pictures, and so on. How should I deal with this? It's simple. Acknowledge feedback, and be open to ideas, and head on to the chapter "Learn the art of selective listening". Acknowledge that there is always a better version. Had it not been the case, Apple would have stopped at the first version of iPhone, Microsoft would have stopped at Windows 3.1, and phones wouldn't have become smart. So, it's time for me to invoke my own journey, fuel the motivation for the next edition of this book, ignore criticism, and incorporate ideas from constructive feedback. I know this sounds arrogant right now, but it is in line with another chapter "Give examples that connect" which talks about cutting things short by giving examples right on the edge to make the desired impact. Also note that this arrogance is not to be spoken and demonstrated, but to be kept within, for your own inspiration.

Remember that "arrogance you deserve" isn't about looking down on others or being over-confident. It's about standing tall on the shoulders of your hard work. It's about knowing your worth and confidently owning your expertise. It's the self-belief that navigates you to even greater heights.

"There is a thin line between confidence and over-confidence. You must be grounded enough to know when you are crossing over."

14

Keep teams engaged

A project usually consists of people from diverse skill sets, different educational backgrounds, and varying degrees of skills. It is this raw talent that must be channelized and kept energized during the project to get the best of their effort. A cricket team, for example, consists of a chosen eleven players, each one carefully selected for a definite purpose. Now imagine if one of the players is not performing optimally. It obviously puts other team members under pressure and ultimately, although in some cases the team wins, it may not always be without those anxious moments. Similarly, when working on complex projects, with challenges looming large and with the need for solutions to intricate problems, keeping every single team member charged is extremely important.

Projects usually start with vigor, everyone is charged up, but once the dust settles down, team leaders tend to get sucked in their own pressures, and team members get carried away in the routine flow, sometimes directionless, and the energy levels can be seen diminishing. As a manager or leader, it is in your own interest to make sure your team is optimally charged up and delivering their best. Being a collection of humans, it is a game of emotions which you must play to perfection. Once you have an engaged team in place, your own performance gets a massive multiplier.

The secret lies not in conducting marathon meetings, giving emotionally charged speeches, putting undue pressure or overwhelming teams with fancy keywords and buzzwords; it's about creating an environment where every member feels seen, valued, and empowered.

Here's how you can go about keeping your teams engaged regardless of your position in the organization.

✔ Show the big picture. Irrespective of what work you allocate to your team, the first step is to paint a vivid picture of the purpose and landscape of the project, and their role in the big picture.

✔ Recognize that everyone, right from a seasoned veteran to an eager intern, wants to see their piece of work materialize. Show them where their work fits in and how it impacts the big picture.

✔ Focus on igniting creative potential through stimulating challenges within the project's framework, instead of just assigning tasks and asking for status updates as a mechanical process. Giving your team the freedom to brainstorm, explore, and feel the joy of discovery, can work wonders.

✔ Keep a watchful eye and become an active mentor, give comfort, and make sure your team is always on the right track. Make sure your team isn't left directionless.

✔ Adopt pen and paper approach to explain key concepts to your team and level them up with your thinking so that you can spawn parallel processes.

✔ Avoid micromanagement. Instead, empower your team with ownership and decision-making within set boundaries. Micromanagement limits initiative, while trust, on the other hand, invokes a sense of responsibility.

✔ Criticize, but also appreciate wholeheartedly. In the present times, we are driven towards being more critical than appreciative. The moment we are asked for a review, the critic in us stands up with suggestions such as "They could have done it in this way", "What's the fun in using this color", "He should have kept it short". We miss appreciating what has been done, and instead focus on what is missing.

✔ Strive to be 80 percent leader who walks alongside, celebrates wins, offers support during setbacks, and 20 percent manager to ensure monitoring and controlling.

Remember that your team's energy translates into your efficiency. If you have disengaged members in your team, it will not only reduce overall productivity but will also increase pressure on others. Hence, adopt the above techniques and have a highly engaged team, motivated, and bubbling with energy.

"Change is all that we seek constantly; lack of that can lead to a lull feeling."

15
Motivate yourself

Motivation is a silent spark within us that ignites us to drive "ourselves" further. Sometimes we feel really charged up to do something, but at times this drive is taken over by lethargy. You may have the intent, but the action is missing. The spark can seem like a candle flickering in the wind, completely unsure about itself. Have you noticed that when we light a candle, the flame keeps switching sides when there is a breeze? You can feel the vulnerable state. Our inner spark is just like that. It keeps fluctuating as a natural response to the external factors around our lives. But the good news is that just like the candle's flame can be stabilized by shielding it from the wind, we can turn our own flickering spark into a roaring flame, and we call this self-motivation.

We all experience a dip in enthusiasm at times, and there is nothing bad about it, as this is a natural process. People often say, "I am down on motivation", "I am feeling demoralized", "I don't feel anything exciting", and express their mental state through similar emotions. When you feel a dip in enthusiasm, the first step is to acknowledge and accept that you are indeed down on morale. Once you are "aware" that you are down on inspiration, consider this as your first victory, as you know at least that there is a problem that needs attention! If you don't know that you are demotivated, and someone else observes it, then it's a different story. In that case you need someone else to motivate you. But here we are talking about a more common scenario in which you know that you are demotivated.

Since you know that you are demotivated, why would you need someone else to motivate you? The truth is motivation lives within you. It is just waiting to be invoked. When you say, "I need a boost", recognize that it is the inner signal provoking you to reignite the fire within you. Now the question is how do you motivate yourself?

Here's how you can go about reigniting the fire and motivating yourself to be at your best once again:

- Treat every adversity as a challenge. When you see things not going your way, it means that your comfort zone is being challenged. Step outside your comfort zone. Acquire a new skill even if it has a steeper learning curve. Getting immersed in a challenge can be a great motivator.

- Set a goal. Without knowing the destination, a journey can best be described as aimless wandering. Without a specific goal or endpoint, the path that you take may lack direction and purpose. You get charged up only when you know that you are set out to reach a destination. Hence, set a target. "See the big picture", "Have smaller milestones with tangible outcomes", and see your motivation fueled up when you achieve each of these milestones!

- Follow an integrated approach. When you fill in air in a balloon, you don't choose to inflate any area of the balloon, it fills as an entire unit. Similarly, your mind experiences a wholistic shift when you choose to pursue a target and celebrate each milestone. You can set any target, such as nurturing a hobby, learning a new skill, finding solution to a specific problem in your profession, or improving a relation. It will all work towards uplifting the state of your mind in its entirety.

- Maintain consistency. Persist with your goal by making it a part of your routine. Schedule dedicated time for your goals. Don't excuse yourself. Consistency is the key to building and maintaining momentum.

- Look back to look ahead. When you feel uninspired at times, recall your achievements from the past. Take a trip down memory lane and live through the moments once again. Live through your achievements, the hurdles that you overcame, the goals you met, and ignite the missing fire once again.

✔ Don't wait for someone to come and motivate you. Realize that it's within you and only you can help yourself more than anyone else.

"Even in moments of weakness, you hold the most powerful tool, the fire within you."

16

Be in control of your project

Delegation is an essential tool when you are working in a team and you have someone reporting to you so that you get the time to work on something higher up, leaving the operational tasks to be handled by your subordinates. It also allows you to leverage the expertise of others, get yourself free time for strategy planning, and at the same time inculcate a sense of ownership within your team. However, effective delegation isn't simply assigning tasks and hoping for the best. It is about striking a balance between empowering your team and maintaining control of the project's overall direction and success.

You will find that projects, irrespective of size, budget, or complexity, are inherently always neck-to-neck. Your planning usually considers the capacity and abilities of your team members, and hence it is natural for you to feel confident when you delegate key project tasks. With this trust you delegate important activities. You feel confident in your team's abilities. Weeks pass by and you find yourself struggling with deadlines staring at you, deliverables not to be seen, and communication feels elusive. These are the dangers of unchecked delegation. Losing control can lead to missed deadlines, quality compromise, and ultimately, project failure.

The key lies in finding the right balance between "letting go" and "holding the reins". Here's how you can delegate activities and still be in control of your project.

- See the big picture. Have a clear understanding of the solution outline of your project, in view of the assumptions, and constraints.

- Clearly define tasks and expectations, and maintain a checklist of deliverables, deadlines, and quality considerations.

- Empower team members but avoid micro-management. It will only hamper their initiative and creativity. Remember to empower, but not neglect!

✔ Don't just delegate tasks; delegate ownership. Brief team members on the project's overall goals and how their specific task contributes to the bigger picture.

✔ Trust your team's expertise but make yourself available to provide timely guidance.

✔ Keep a Plan-B ready to be able to make a swift switch if you observe things not going the right way in the present approach.

✔ Perform a periodic probe test to identify and address issues early on, course-correct if needed, and ensure deliveries are on track.

✔ Don't let delegating overshadow communication with your client. Maintain regular communication with your client, keeping them informed about progress and addressing any concerns.

17

Someone must do the actual work; you be the one

Whenever there are brainstorming sessions, you'll often see many ideas flowing in. It is commonly said that "Ideas are bundant, but execution is scarce". Many teams fall prey to this "execution gap", which occurs when the enthusiasm for new ideas outshines the commitment to their implementation. Marathon brainstorming sessions with innovative techniques on how to conduct productive meetings often generate excitement, but without dedicated people who can translate those ideas into tangible actions, the discussions remain as "masterpiece on paper".

I'm sure you must have come across similar situations at your workplace, or even in your personal life. You will always see an influx of ideas, advice, and suggestions, but little takers when it comes to bringing the idea to life! When you are part of a team, it is natural for everyone to contribute their thoughts and ideas. After all, thinking and proposing something does not amount to own commitment. However, it is important to ensure that someone is stepping up to execute those ideas. This is where you can seize the opportunity – to be that person who takes on the responsibility of translating plans into action, the one who does the actual work.

Fearlessness, commitment, and the willingness to take responsibility are the essential qualities of the one who chooses to do the actual work, irrespective of obstacles or challenges. Instead of waiting for others to take the lead, seize the opportunity to be the driving force, empower yourself to take charge and make things happen. You must roll up your sleeves and get your hands dirty and set yourself apart by doing the actual work.

Working at the grassroot level also gives you a greater advantage of having complete hands-on knowledge of your project. A late entrant to your project may not be able to relate to the intricacies that you have worked up through several rounds of trials and errors.

So, next time you see a lot of discussion happening, try to "find the starting point" and just dive in. It will be challenging, but it will also be a lot of fun.

If you aren't a "doer" already, here's how you can become one:

- If you sense an opportunity, seize it.

- Take the initiative with a keen willingness to get your hands dirty.

- Do not let the fear of failure creep up leading to procrastination and inaction.

- Try to hold yourself accountable for success or failure.

- Don't let setbacks deter you; learn from them, adapt, and persist in your efforts.

- Inspire others along the way.

"Your expressions determine how far you reach in pursuit of your aspirations… Stay positive and embrace all challenges."

18

Save 90 minutes a day with smart work

We all have the same 24 hours in a day, but some seem to make the most of it with what they call a "massive twenty-four hours." This is clear from their lifestyle, how well they balance work and life, even with more work and parallel activities to juggle. For most of us the clock ticks relentlessly, and the pressure to finish work keeps mounting. While some seem to conquer mountains of tasks, others find themselves struggling in the deep sea of mounting list of "to do". Have you ever pondered over why this inequality exists?

The trick lies in reclaiming 90 minutes of precious time every day with smart work. Wouldn't it be a great accomplishment if you could earn yourself a whopping 90 minutes every day? The good news is, especially if your work involves computers, it doesn't require any superhuman effort, but it's just with smart work that you can achieve using everyday tools.

If you examine a typical day, you will often come across something or the other that can be classified into "mundane" activities. There are hundreds of such tasks that might be going unnoticed. Here's a sample, and I'm sure you will be able to find out similarities, either in your routine, or as one-off tasks.

- Copying and pasting content from emails.
- Copying data from a website and formatting it in Excel sheet.
- Editing hundreds of PDF files and saving them in a folder structure.
- Renaming thousands of picture files.
- Converting documents from one file format to another.
- Formatting and printing address labels for mailing.
- Consolidating multiple Excel files into a single master spreadsheet.
- Generating personalized mail merge documents for mass communication.
- Setting up identical software on several computer systems.
- Verifying backups from multiple computers.

- Creating personalized greeting cards or certificates.

Here's how you can go about reclaiming your precious 90 minutes.

✔ The first thing that you should do when you start using any software is to just go through the complete menu structure and all the options available. This won't help much at first but will give you an idea of the boundaries of the application so that you know if there exists a better and smarter way to handle something.

✔ Make extensive use of simple editors such as Notepad or Notepad++ as intermediate passthrough. These can be especially useful when you copy formatted content and paste it as unformatted or plain text in Excel or Word. Although options such as "Paste Special" are available in Microsoft products, having Notepad as an intermediate editor can be a great productivity booster.

✔ Find and use keyboard shortcuts for frequent operations. For instance, using "Ctrl-C" is way more effective than right clicking the mouse button and selecting "Copy" option. Similarly pressing "F5" for refresh is much faster than right clicking and selecting the option to refresh.

✔ Learn Excel Macros and VBA scripting. This will open a massive gateway to great productivity hacks. The power of VBA is such that you can drastically reduce your engagement time from weeks to days, and days to hours.

✔ Explore the power of formulae in Excel such as VLOOKUP and XLOOKUP. If you are dealing with multiple but related datasets, these can certainly relieve you from tedious manual comparison tasks.

The above is just indicative of how you can invoke what you already possess. For example, F5 as a shortcut for refresh always existed, but you may not have invoked it. The idea is to keep your eyes wide open and be mindful of what you are doing and how. Question each of your actions. Ask yourself, "Is this the most efficient way?". Make yourself feel uncomfortable if you find yourself doing something repetitively or doing something in multiple steps. Question your beliefs and make the discomfort fire you up to reclaim 90 minutes of your day, one action at a time!

19

Understand that stress is just a state of mind

I am under a lot of stress; "I'm feeling stressed out"; "There's too much of workload and I'm completely stressed"; "The stress is really getting to me"; "I'm feeling really overwhelmed by all of this".

Do these emotions sound familiar in your work or personal life? With looming deadlines, piling workloads and tremendous pressure concerning work, finance, relationships, and so many other factors, stress has now become an omnipresent foe.

Our perception of events plays a significant role in what we consider as "stress" and how much stress we experience. A situation that one person finds overwhelming might be met with calm determination by another. Our thoughts, beliefs, and interpretations of situations significantly influence our emotional responses. For instance, an upcoming presentation might trigger anxiety in one person, leading to a racing heart and sweaty palms. However, another person might view the same presentation as an opportunity to showcase their skills, resulting in great motivation.

While external circumstances can contribute to stress, it's important to recognize the significant role our perceptions and interpretations play. The same event can trigger varying degrees of stress in different people, depending on their mindset. Thus, stress is not an external force, rather it is just an interpretation of the situation resulting in a certain state of our own mind, and since it is a state of mind, the good news is that we can influence it and disrupt the stress response.

Even with the ability to influence our stress response, neglecting it can have serious consequences. Chronic stress can lead to burnout, anxiety, depression, and even physical health problems that can surface in forms never imagined.

Our mind usually signals either "fight" or "fly". Those who know how to deal with the situation fight and eventually win over, while others just flee away. Let's see how we can get into the first category and fight it out.

✔ When you notice stress creeping in, acknowledge it. Acceptance is the first step towards finding solutions. Once accepted, commit to halting negative thoughts and replacing them with positive ones.

✔ Apply multiple forces of positive energy by rephrasing all the negative thoughts that come to your mind into positive notes. For example, instead of thinking "I'm going to fail", you can rephrase it as "I know it's difficult, but I take it as a challenge, and this is my opportunity to win". When there are multiple sources of positive vibes, you will notice that stress already begins to weaken.

✔ Stress is not an event, but a ripple effect of all that has accumulated over a period. Hence, deep breathing is something that can bring immediate calm and allow some peace to emerge.

✔ Read the chapter "Learn the art of compartmentalizing" and practice the art so that you don't overthink about something that's causing all the stress, and at the same time give yourself some breathing space.

✔ Stress is a state of the mind, hence engage your mind in something you really enjoy, such as a hobby, a sport, experimenting in the kitchen, or anything (that isn't addictive) that you feel can help de-stress and recharge.

✔ Talk to someone you trust, someone who will listen to you and share some inspiration with a positive outlook, but not someone that will sympathize and aggravate your stress further.

"Stay conscious and logical at all times; it is very easy for your mind to believe in something that never was."

20

Nurture a hobby

We all are busy with work, and often ignore how important it is to nurture our hobbies. Yet, these seemingly offtrack activities play a big role in keeping our minds healthy and thus, can really help us perform at our peak. Hobbies give us a way to let go of negative thoughts and fill our life with happiness, creativity, and a sense of achievement in routine chaos. We all need a break from our daily routine. Hobbies do just that. They help us refresh and find ourselves again. Our days typically are loaded with an infinite list of to-dos, and taking time for hobbies may seem like a luxury. On the contrary, however, it is like investing in our own well-being.

So, once you acknowledge that your life has become a slave to your routine, take a moment to let that feeling sink in. You will realize that you are not in control of yourself, rather circumstances are demanding you to dance to random tunes, away from the desires of your inner self. We all have an intrinsic child in us, the one that finds happiness in seeing us immersed in the "seemingly offtrack" activities. However, we silence that child unknowingly, and let it starve for what it truly deserves. Now is the time to wake up. Look back at yourself. Find what you like doing away from your routine, where you find happiness.

If you are finding yourself too consumed by your professional obligations, you can still find a way to open a playground for your own self, and here's how you can go about it.

- Know yourself. Know what really charges you up. It could be a form of art like singing, dancing, painting, or any creative art; It could be writing, blogging, vlogging; It could be research and experimentation; It could be a sport, or anything else that makes you happy.

- You must focus on being a creator and not just a passive taker of what others make. You can divide your free time 80:20, wherein you can allow 20 percent of your time in consuming, while 80 percent goes in creating. For example, although you may say that you find happiness in reading, watching TV, listening to podcasts, web series, or scrolling through social feeds, limit it to just 20 percent. Invest 80 percent of your free time in activities such as learning a new skill, pursuing a passion project, or engaging in a sport or a creative idea, as that will be more satisfying.

- You must dedicate a time slot for your hobby. Head on to "Treat everything as primary activity" and make sure to take your hobby seriously!

- Don't look for profit or loss in a hobby. When you engage in a hobby, understand that it is primarily for yourself, for your own happiness. Hence, if you are questioned about what monetary gains you are going to make out of it, choose not to get distracted by such questions. The first step is to just engage yourself for the sake of healing the scars on your mind created by your busy schedule.

- Limit your effort on hobby activities to 20 percent. When you start working on your hobby, just go for it. Don't overthink, especially on the aspect of financial gain. See the big picture of how far you can go, what all you can achieve, and work towards it, but don't convert your hobby into your daily routine right at the first step.

- Find a new hobby. Let's say you get deeply engrossed in a hobby that you found from the effort above, so much so that you made that the purpose of your life. Now, this being your daily routine, you'll certainly have setbacks, pressures and all that makes you feel the desire to find time for yourself. What do you do? Simple. Nurture a new hobby!

"Doing what you like is freedom, liking what you do is happiness, and innovating in whatever you do is enjoyment."

21
Identify your leadership spot

Leadership. The word probably makes you think of bosses telling people what to do from cabins exercising their authority, or sports stars cheering their teams. What if you were asked to believe that leadership isn't something reserved for a privileged few?

Do you feel a different energy when explaining a complex concept to a friend or a colleague? Or maybe, do you find yourself being looked up to when a project needs a creative spark? Leadership isn't confined to boundaries. It's a powerful force that can reside within anyone, waiting to be unleashed. The key lies in identifying your unique leadership "spot" – that special place where your talents and passions converge, igniting a fire that inspires and empowers others.

When you are working in a large group, it is quite natural to get overwhelmed by the towering experience or seniors, the aura of talented colleagues, the brilliance of a fresher, and so on. There is just so much happening around, you might just feel yourself holding back, not sure if you would ever get to see yourself stand out in the crowd.

Wait! Believe in your capabilities.

You must believe that you have at least one quality in your arsenal that's unique to you. You have a spark that nobody else has. You are the master in something that your manager, colleague, or subordinate isn't. It could be anything – your writing skills, your listening skills, crisis management, relations management, singing, dancing, physique, cooking, scripting, mentalism, social media – this list can go on and on! It's not about emulating the style of someone else; it's about identifying your own brand of brilliance.

Until you know yourself, you are like a dormant volcano that's brimming with immense potential. Just like the volcano needs a spark to erupt and transform its raw potential into a powerful force, your "leadership spot" within is waiting to erupt and anchor your career. Observe yourself and ignite your potential.

If you haven't discovered yourself yet, or if you have discovered but haven't anchored your life around it yet, here's what you can do.

- Know yourself. Acknowledge the unique strengths that you are naturally good at. Think of all that makes you come alive. May be its your enthusiasm, laser-sharp focus, optimism, humor in the face of adversity. Just make a list of all that differentiates you.

- Carve a niche for yourself so that people are drawn to your authenticity and inspired by your passion.

- Don't wait for the "perfect opportunity", it doesn't always come knocking. Instead, look for ways to knit your strengths in everyday life. For example, in a heavy technology-oriented project, if you sense that an Excel macro can save days of work, and you happen to be an Excel wizard, go ahead, and offer your expertise. Remember, every interaction is a chance to share your spark.

- Celebrate the ripple effect of your success and continue expanding the horizon of your unique skills.

Solutions are present right under the nose, but we ignore what we have and wander in search elsewhere. Do the following simple exercise while you are reading this. Look through your window and notice everything around you, both near and far. What did you see? Probably the trees, buildings, cars, and people? Chances are that you did not notice what's right in front of you, the very first thing you see through the window - the window glass, or the grilles! Hence, see what you have first, exploit its complete potential, and build on it.

"Back yourself when things are not going your way, and back others when things are not going their way."

22

Do not hesitate to experiment

Let's say you are in a typical 9 – 6 job routine, doing the same mundane activity, and following this routine day after day. It need not be a mundane activity per se, might as well be a highly skilled work. But, without anything new and exciting, wouldn't boredom take over? You might have reached a mountain peak once, twice, thrice using a familiar well-trodden path, but what if there was an alternative route, going through the valleys, offering breathtaking scenic views? That's the essence of experimentation.

We are influenced by our past experiences and hence habituated to finding comfort in predictable routines. Although the proven methods have worked for us in the past, clinging too tightly to the familiar methods can become a trap, limit our creativity, problem-solving abilities, and ultimately, deprive us of extraordinary achievement. If you look at your own life, you'll see a definite pattern, a pattern that is built on familiar methods, technologies, and even people. This path has been your guide all along, but since it is like a tunnel, all your thoughts circle inside the tunnel, and hence at some point, progress seems to stall.

Think about how you find technology solutions, design business models, or the way you handle teams. For example, if you have designed successful software earlier in your career, chances are you will utilize the same structure for your next projects. Has the world moved on? Can there be a better alternative? How often do you say, "let me experiment"?

Experimentation is the act of stepping off the beaten path, of questioning "what if?" It's about trying new things, exploring different approaches, and taking on the unknown, igniting curiosity, and venturing into uncharted waters to discover hidden gems. Apply the experimenting method in your work, especially when you feel stalled in a situation, and you'll find solutions automatically.

If you are finding yourself reluctant, here are some pointers to get you started with experimenting:

✔ Experiment with technology. The world of technology is constantly evolving. Don't be afraid to try new tools, software, or platforms. You might just stumble upon a game changer.

✔ Experiment with your methods. There are countless ways to approach a problem. Experiment with unconventional approaches, and you might find a solution that others overlooked. Take a pen and paper, draw a circle and jot down your tried methods in that circle. Then write down new approaches out of the circle. That's your infinite playground for experimentation.

✔ Experiment with partners and vendors. Step outside of your established comfort zone in terms of vendors. Explore new partnerships, collaborations, and service providers. They might bring a fresh perspective. You may get better deals, comfortable payment terms, and better service.

✔ Experiment with people. Surround yourself with people from diverse backgrounds. People who challenge your assumptions often inspire new ways of thinking. Working with people from diverse backgrounds and disciplines and out of the box views of such people can be the trigger of innovation.

✔ Experiment in the kitchen. Even the seemingly mundane act of cooking can be a playground for experimentation. The success of trying out new ingredients and combining flavors in unexpected ways can translate into other areas of your life as well.

✔ Experiment with Google. Searching with the same set of keywords and context will fetch you the same results with different variations. Break free and search beyond the obvious, by exploring long tail keywords, and you will find new clues. Experiment with search operators such as site:, inurl:, intitle:, ext:, and more.

✔ Experiment with yourself. Don't be afraid to step outside your comfort zone and try new things, even if they seem unrelated to your current goals. Learn something new, do something differently, and this can open doors to unexpected discoveries and hidden talents within yourself.

"Repetitions are boring, frustrating, and depressing; new is interesting and exciting; Same applies to mistakes; experiment and make plenty of them, but new and exciting each time.

23

Commit to your commitment

Dedicating yourself to fulfilling your promises or obligations, irrespective of the size, context, or complexity means committing to your commitment. As it involves your "word", it is your responsibility to stay true to it. Essentially, it means that you must remain persistent and determined to honor the commitments you have made. There will be challenges along the way, but you will have to find innovative ways to surpass them and fulfill the commitments you have made.

In the fast-paced world, there is an urge to seize every opportunity, and the inner pressure to say "yes", the key drivers being competition, pressure imposed by circumstances, and the fear of missing out (FOMO). However, when you say yes to something, you must consider the larger implications, the greatest being that you would be betting on your own word. It is thus important to think twice and commit once.

Here's how you can sail through the journey of your commitment.

- Do not rush to commit in the heat of the moment. Take your time instead to pause, reflect, and ask yourself if you're ready to stand by it, and promise only when you are absolutely sure.

- Insist on buying some time to help yourself lay the groundwork as a solid foundation of your commitment. Invest time and effort in understanding all the intricacies. Gather information, plan meticulously, identify the boundaries, and set realistic expectations.

- Strive to honor your commitment. Your word is the most precious jewel that you possess, hence never let it down. Once you have made a commitment, honor it with complete integrity.

- Every commitment, irrespective of size, impact and purpose is equally important. Hence, treat every commitment, whether in personal life or in a corporate environment, with equal importance. These are the actions that contribute to building your character and reputation of trustworthiness. Thus, whether it is about delivering a project within schedule or simply showing up on time, both assume the same level of significance.

✔ Put in the extra effort, time, dedication, learn whatever is required, and travel the extra mile to honor your commitment as that sets you apart and demonstrates your willingness to bridge the gap between intent and action.

✔ Commitment is an attitude, practice it through baby steps in daily life.

"Commit to yourself before you commit to anyone else."

24

Maintain a comfortable posture

Speed and pressure are a hallmark of the modern work culture. We push ourselves to such an extent that unknowingly, we tend to give our own body the last priority, rather we take it for granted. We simply ignore the signals our body tries to convey. Perceiving ourselves to be deeply engrossed in a busy schedule, we prefer visiting the doctor hoping for a magic pill when there is a problem versus observing ourselves as a routine measure and making minor corrections.

Take a break right now and observe yourself. Do you feel physical discomfort anywhere – strain on eyes, a niggle in wrist, pain in neck, stiffness in back, or tightness in knee? If yes, these are the signals that your body is "requesting" you to correct, by not doing something out of the way, but by just tweaking the way you sit, type, read, and travel. Whispers like these are your silent performance chokers and you must listen to them right away to prevent them from becoming the chronic problems of tomorrow.

Here are some very easy tips that you can simply observe and correct if needed:

✔ Desk alignment. Check out if your keyboard or laptop is properly aligned with the edges of your desk. If it isn't aligned, then probably you are typing with one hand stretched causing strain on multiple muscles.

✔ Keyboard height. Check the height of your keyboard. Ensure you have a base good enough to give comfort to your wrist.

✔ Mouse placement. Pay attention to the placement of the mouse. If it is too near the edge of the desk or too far away from the keyboard, then you may be struggling with the movement.

- External mouse. If you are using a laptop, prefer using an external mouse over the inbuilt trackpad for better performance gain.

- Neck posture. Avoid putting too much pressure on your neck. Keep it relaxed and aligned with your spine to prevent discomfort and potential issues going forward.

- Weight distribution. Ensure equal distribution of weight on both sides of your body, whether sitting or standing. This helps in better alignment and reduces the risk of strain.

- Computer screen. Do not ignore if the screen color looks unusual, blurry, or flickering. Ensure the brightness is just right enough, not too dull and not too bright.

- Handrest height. Maintain "just right" height of the handrests of your chair to support your arms and shoulders. Make sure both the sides are at the same height.

- When carrying a bag on your back, ensure the straps are balanced to distribute the weight evenly to minimize strain on your shoulders and spine during travel. Check your bag now if both straps are of equal height!

A clean work environment is an essential component for free flow of ideas. Hence, take care of your device and your work setup. Spare just five minutes to clean your desk, screen, keyboard, and surface of the mouse. Apart from looking clean and hygienic, it will also give you a sense of involvement and ownership.

"Stay attuned to yourself, listen to your body, and experience longevity."

25

Inform in advance

One exciting chapter in this book is called "Spring a Surprise." It's all about doing something unexpected that brings out the best in you, leaving everyone surprised. You'll learn how to make your mark by disrupting anticipative tendencies. However, surprises don't always work in your favor, especially in situations where others are dependent on you, and that's where the immensely impactful skill, the skill of informing in advance, comes into play.

Sometimes there are situations where you expect some crucial piece of information from a subordinate for your presentation. The deadline has passed, and you haven't heard a word. You are left anxious in uncertainty. Is the report done? Will it be ready in time? Should you scramble to find an alternative? This feeling of being kept in the dark is not only stressful, but also impacts your own focus. Now examine the emotions that you generate in this short span - Anxiety, Uncertainty, Impatience, Helplessness, Stress, Frustration, Doubt, Disappointment, Distrust. While five of these emotions depict your state of mind, the remaining four directly tag your colleague, creating a particular perception that can potentially have a long-term impact depending on the severity of the situation.

Imagine you were in that position, responsible for delivering those reports to your manager. You tried your best to deliver the report in a way that could have had a significant impact, however just because you failed to inform your manager about the delay, it could have consequences that you never imagined.

This is where the art of proactive communication comes into picture, as the price of waiting could have domino effects that you've never imagined. You can take a moment here, and quickly run through the recent past, where you found yourself caught up, or lead someone else to be tangled in similar situations. If your answer is affirmative, then you must follow the pointers given below to start proactive communication as a strategy. The following are just indicative ideas, and you can always devise your own based on your own experience.

- Anticipate project or task delays? Even a slight delay can cause a ripple effect. A quick heads-up allows others to adjust their schedules and expectations, minimizing disruption.

- Running late for a meeting? A message beforehand prevents wasted waiting time and wasted energy for others.

- Do you see potential roadblocks? Share such challenges to keep everyone on the same page and make way for collaborative problem-solving.

- Are you changing your plans? Don't do this on the fly assuming others to automatically adapt to your plans. Inform them well in advance so that they can alter theirs.

Proactive communication also works wonders in personal life. Imagine waiting for a special surprise promised by a friend, only to find yourself waiting all day long. You start feeling worried about what happened, wondering if you were a victim of some mischief. You might start feeling impatient and stressed, not knowing what to do. It's frustrating when plans don't unfold as expected, and doubts begin to surface.

"Communicate in time to take out the guesswork."

26

Spring a surprise

Humans, by design, are programmed to anticipate outcomes, and that is also an inherent tendency. We all gather clues and process those subconsciously, correlate with past experiences, and form our expectations. This then becomes our own mental framework for further interactions. When you are given an assignment, there is an implicit expectation for it to be completed in a specific manner. This task can be anything from creating a new design, preparing a presentation, creating reports, and so on.

You can disrupt this framework by choosing a path distant from "run-of-the-mill" by setting new benchmarks and exceeding expectations, triggering a positive surprise that registers as "impressive" and memorable.

One of the key aspects of peak performance is traversing beyond the obvious, and exceeding expectations. Not just exceeding expectations, but surprising through your innovative approaches for a lasting impression. Consistency builds trust, but it is the unexpected surge of positive surprises that stands you out in the crowd.

Surprises can be as trivial as formatting a document in a way that nobody else in your team has done before; or attending a meeting with detailed design when all that was expected was a simple approach document; or sudden rollout of a complex idea that you had been working on in hours when only the owls are active.
So, work on a surprise, and see the difference it makes in the attitude of how you are looked at!

Here's how you can spring a surprise:

- Master the art of observation. You must develop a keen eye for detail and "read between the lines". You will get clues simply by being an active listener. When you actively listen to conversations with your clients or colleagues, you will get to know their pain points without you explicitly asking, or their telling explicitly. You must anticipate these and tailor your approach to exceed the expectations that they never spoke of.

✔ Think differently. You don't have to settle for the "good enough" or simply the expected solution. Challenge yourself to think outside the box, explore unconventional methods, leverage hidden resources, and propose solutions that address underlying issues, not just the surface problems.

✔ Anticipate problems and keep solutions ready. As an actively immersed member of a project, you must continuously assess your projects to anticipate potential roadblocks. Once you are aware of the foreseen challenges, you can work on solutions and present those before the problems even surface.

✔ Deliver with excellence. Surprises are like double edged swords. They have all the capability to make or break, depending on the outcome. Hence, when you choose to surprise, make it a point to ensure that it is well executed and with excellence.

✔ Work on surprises in everyday life. As we are talking about an integrated approach to peak performance, the playing field of surprises goes beyond our professional routine and extends to everyday life. For example, you can present greetings and gifts in innovative ways that transcend the traditional approach; or go beyond sympathy with a genuine intent to help someone in need; volunteer in opportunities that show a different and unexpected version of you!

By incorporating these strategies into your daily life, you can cultivate the habit of exceeding expectations and leave a positive and lasting impression on those around you. Remember, it's the little surprises, delivered with thoughtfulness and intent, that can truly set the right perceptions about you.

"Shrug off what you believe to be yourself and you will discover a new and exciting you."

27

Learn the art of selective listening

If you analyze a typical day, it is filled with advice, opinions, emails, social media, meetings, and endless conversations. But when you are in beast mode, you don't have to listen to it all. In fact, you can't listen to it all. That's where the art of selective listening comes in.

Our brain is a high-powered computer. It can process only the amount of information which it is designed for. When you overload it with irrelevant details, it slows down, obstructing your ability to focus and perform at your best. Selective listening functions as the firewall of your mental bandwidth, allowing only the most crucial information to enter and process. Furthermore, 80 per cent of the information that enters is filled with emotions and only 20 per cent comprise objective data. The moment your mind carries those emotions, it is a writing on the wall that your performance is going to suffer.

Remember, everyone gets only 24 hours, or a whole t-w-e-n-t-y f-o-u-r hours. To truly make the most of your day, selective listening acts as a powerful tool, allowing you to focus on specific points amidst the subjective chatter. Compare this with an orchestra that has several instruments playing their unique sounds. You can choose to listen to the symphony of sounds in entirety, which is the default function, or with extra effort you'll be able to focus on one instrument such as the Guitar while filtering out the sounds of Violin, Drums, and others. Put on your earphones and listen to your favorite music. Try it once, and you'll experience a different kind of satisfaction!

Selective listening is an art, and here's how it can be practiced and mastered in our daily routine:

✔ Every interaction deserves a purpose. Are you in a meeting to brainstorm or receive updates? Know your goal to help tune into relevant information and politely excuse yourself from irrelevant sidetracks. This doesn't always have to be an explicit statement of exit.

Just like you filter out instruments in an orchestra, you can keep your ears listening on the points of interest and utilize the "noise time" for thinking about your unfinished tasks. Read the chapter "Learn and practice multitasking" to get ideas on how you can utilize this time.

✔ Valuable insights deserve your attention, while empty chatter must be muted. Working on developing the discernment muscle can help, as it is with this ability that you'll be able to distinguish between a well-informed critique and an empty chatter. The best way to develop discernment muscle is by summarizing your own day and reflecting on the subjective and objective talks that you did during the day.

✔ Unending discussions often laced with emotion, can cloud the core message, and only lead to waste of time and energy. Just listening to an emotional outburst can take a serious toll on your mental health. Hence, uncover the context. Cut things short. Ask yourself, what led to this conversation? What does the other person want me to understand? Once you get clarity, drive the conversation towards the solution with a positive mindset.

✔ A conversation need not be continuous tit-for-tat, word for a word. You can pause on your turn in the conversation, process information, and ask clarifying questions to ensure you are in tune with the context.

✔ Your focus is precious, scattered emails only dilute it. . As you climb the organizational ladder, you'll find yourself CC'd on endless email chains. You can't really do anything about it. Hence, unless your involvement is crucial, just give a quick scan and move on.

✔ Meetings shouldn't be marathons. Go prepared with an agenda, focus on clear communication "devoid of emotions", and aim for a defined outcome. Shorter, focused meetings save your time as well as keep your team engaged and productive. Remember, "selective speaking" indirectly eliminates the need for selective listening.

✓ Observe stereograms. They can give you great perspectives from the noise which in raw form looks nothing more than obfuscated garbage. Looking at stereograms sharpens your ability to make meaning out of clutter. Apply the same to your meetings and conversations and see the magic unfold! Decode the stereograms given at the end of this chapter as an exercise in selective listening.

Here's how you can decode a stereogram:

1. Try to see them one at a time initially.

2. Position yourself by holding the stereogram at a comfortable distance, roughly at eye level.

3. Change your eye focus through techniques such as diverging and crossing eyes.

4. Tweak the distance if required. A distance of 1 – 2 feet will generally work.

5. Be curious and break the mental bias to see the hidden secrets!

Selective listening isn't about ignoring others. It's about being present in the moment, actively focusing on what matters most.

"You pass the real test of your mental focus when you stare at a glaring screen and yet see what you wish to see what is projected on the screen."

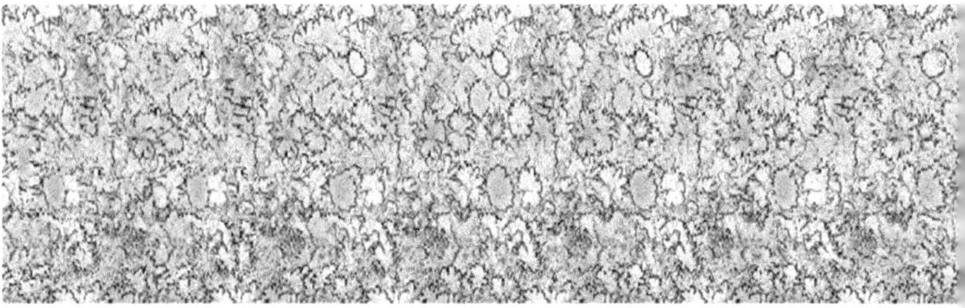

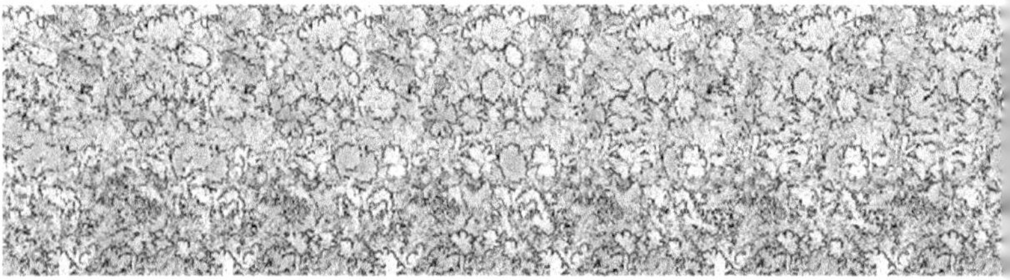

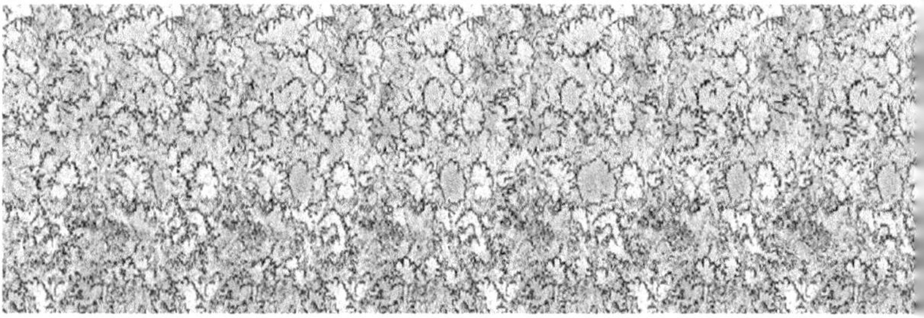

28

Stay ahead in your field

We were in the feature phone era just a few years ago, and those devices have become a thing of the past within the blink of an eye. We have done well to adapt to these advancements. Regardless of the generation that users belong to, they can easily use the latest gadgets with ease. This means we have been massively successful as consumers. But can we say the same thing about ourselves as creators?

May be yes or may be not! Let's say, we talk about programming languages. Back in the old days, we had limited options – database programmers had the option of COBOL or FoxPro, system programmers had the option of Assembly, C & C++, frontend developers had the option of Visual Basic or PowerBuilder, web developers had ASP, Java, or PHP, while mobile developers had Symbian and J2ME. It was easy to choose a path and build a career around it. Today, there are hundreds of libraries, plenty of languages, frameworks, open-source communities, and AI models to choose from. Am I still relevant? That's the question you should ask yourself. Have your skills just outdated and are you overshadowed by the new generation? In the current context, every new graduate is a new generation, thanks to the massive speed of technology development.

The new generation looks up to you as a leader courtesy of your experience or position in an organization, but not essentially due to your technical acumen. It is too easy to decipher the trend and technology gap. But here's a simple strategy to build a perception about you, one that cuts across generations and makes you a natural leader. The key is to stay ahead in your field and remain abreast of developments in associated areas.

If you are already feeling the pressure of being caught up and overtaken, here's something you can start right away:

- Don't stop learning; that's the key. As you climb up the corporate ladder, it is expected of you to groom the next generation, as well as look into the managerial aspect of things. Although you may not be required to perform hands-on tasks, it is a good idea to remain updated about the happenings in your domain of expertise.

- Make it a point to know a thing or two more than anyone else in your team, even if it demands putting in extra time and effort or taking some online courses. You will automatically find ways once you commit yourself to stay ahead of others!

- Don't shy away from exploring new ideas. You may be used to a certain framework and may have gained a good amount of expertise. For example, as a developer, although you may be used to a certain IDE such as NetBeans, it is also worthwhile checking out Visual Studio Code. This is applicable in any field, and the possibilities are limitless; QR Code instead of Barcode, NFC instead of RFID, Cloud instead of On-premises, Doodle instead of stock video, and so on.

- Remain curious. It is the spark that ignites fire within you to learn new things and explore limitless possibilities. Whenever you see something different, don't hesitate to explore it out of curiosity, even if it may not be relevant in the current context.

- Peek into the world of Gen-Z to update yourself with what is trending. For someone belonging to the 20th century, the 21st-century trends might seem rubbish. Yet, it is important to stay updated and align yourself with the latest developments to stay ahead in your field.

- Bring out the best of both worlds. When you perform the above, you will have a hold over the age-old foundational basics as well as be able to employ new trends.

- Participate actively in healthy competition across generations and age groups. Do not shy away from participating in discussion on latest and emerging trends, even though you may feel off-track.

"Dream big, challenge your limits, and live your dream; learn plenty of new things in the process and build your unique library known as experience."

29

Learn the art of unlearning

Learning new things is important to stay current, but equally important is forgetting old, outdated stuff. Unlearning is about cleaning that mental baggage of outdated ideas, habits, bias, and assumptions. Getting rid of past notions makes room for new ways of thinking, new approaches and fresh perspectives altogether.

Unlearning does not simply mean forgetting whatever you have acquired. It is an intricate process that involves introspection and neutral, unbiased assessment. It is an intricate process that involves introspection and neutral unbiased assessment. It is the process of acknowledging that something better exists and for that the old must be given up. It is an art that can be mastered through continuous practice.

Why is unlearning important? Well, to achieve peak performance, it is important that we challenge our beliefs, the ones that we had been following blindly, the ones that we acquired through self-learning, and most importantly, the ones for which we can accept that there exists a better way! Unlearning is the first baby step towards exploring a better way to achieve great results.

Why is unlearning such a challenge? Let me give an example. Consider the vast community of computer users, many of whom would confidently claim proficiency in typing. However, only a small percentage of these would have attended a technical typing course, while a majority would be the self-taught ones. Among these, some may boast impressive speeds of 45 words per minute using just two fingers. Now, if you were to suggest to such a proficient typist that there exists a superior method capable of achieving speeds of 80 words per minute, what would be the reaction? It would often be the one of resistance and skepticism, as you would be directly challenging their deeply ingrained beliefs.

Now, let's envision a scenario where the typist decides to take on the journey of learning to type using all nine fingers, a more technical approach. This marks the onset of internal conflict and resistance. Imagine the first day of practice, with a tough task of mastering the sequence "ASDFGF ;LKJHJ" with nine fingers. Transitioning from a seemingly effortless two-finger technique to a more intricate method involving significantly more fingers is undoubtedly frustrating. Yet, suppose this person manages to overcome this initial hurdle and persists with the process of unlearning and relearning.

There comes a period of distress during this transition phase. The typist finds caught between worlds – no longer able to type at the previous speed of 45 words per minute using the old method, and not yet proficient enough to match even 30 words per minute with the new technical approach. This stage is marked by frustration, uncertainty, and a sense of disorientation as old habits are shed, and new skills are acquired.

Now, this makes unlearning such a difficult process, and there is a tendency to give up.

But what if you keep practicing, even when it's tough? You slowly learn the new finger placements, one keystroke at a time, programming your brain to a new method. It's like building a new muscle memory. And guess what? Eventually, you would be typing way faster and smoother than before!

That's the power of unlearning and relearning. It takes effort, but it can lead to amazing results.

I've chosen to use the example of a typist because there's another chapter in this book called "Learn the art of typing." Typing is one of the most important skills to learn because it frees up a lot of your brain's resources from mechanical tasks that can otherwise be deployed in something that requires a lot of thinking.

Learning typing is just one of the personal development initiatives that no one will force upon you, and an apt case study for unlearning and relearning. However, there are inevitable situations, such as when you switch jobs, and you are forced upon unlearning your old methods of documenting, coding, administration, designing, and adapting to the new ones laid down by the new organization. Begin practicing unlearning right now to develop mental expertise in the concept, ensuring it becomes a valuable skill ready to be utilized when the situation calls for it.

So, embrace unlearning, if you believe there exists a better way. It's hard, but it's worth it.

Here's how you can go about unlearning:

✔ Be open to the possibility that there may be better, more effective ways of doing things.

✔ Maintain a sense of curiosity and a willingness to explore new ideas and perspectives.

✔ Make up your mind to deal with self-resistance.

✔ Visualize yourself unlearning old and learning new techniques to reinforce positive intent.

✔ Acknowledge and celebrate each step forward, whether big or small.

✔ Believe in your capability; you've done this before, and you'll do it better this time!

✔ Be patient; change takes time and it's important to be patient and persistent.

"Unlearning is amongst the toughest of mental exercises. It is stressful but the results are truly rewarding."

30
Learn reporting craftmanship

You may have slogged hard on a project, and the project could have achieved the desired results, or might have failed. In either case, as a protocol, you are required to produce a report of all that has taken place and explain what, why, who, how, when, where, backed by relevant facts and figures. Irrespective of the outcome of the project, this is your opportunity to make the stakeholders perceive your effort in the right frame, which in turn will help boost your quest for peak performance. After all, when someone is watching you from a distance, there is a high probability that the ground reality may significantly differ from what is perceived. Hence, the ability to communicate complex information clearly, concisely, and impactfully assumes great significance in the measurement of your performance. In any field, crafting effective reports is a superpower that separates the merely competent from the truly exceptional.

Reporting is not just about compiling data, rather it is a form of art in which you understand your audience and empower yourself to present information using stories, facts, figures, visuals, meaningful tables, and key outcomes using persuasive methods such that you fulfill the desired objectives. In a professional work environment, whether you are dealing within the organization or with customers, it is important that you master this art, which will help maintain status quo, control adverse situations, or even turn hopeless situations into great opportunities. It's about how you present the facts. Here are some tips to help you craft reports.

✔ Understand your audience. The first step to crafting a compelling report is understanding your audience. Who will be reading it? Are they experts in the field, or do they require a more foundational understanding? What are their specific needs and expectations? Tailoring your language, level of detail, and use of appropriate visual elements ensures your message resonates effectively.

- Formulate a story in your mind. Every report has a purpose. Identify yours. What do you want to achieve? Do you intend to inform a decision, persuade an action, or simply share your findings? Once you are clear with your objective, divide your report into logical sections, each having its own narrative.

- Begin with a summary. Imagine walking into a meeting and immediately launching into a detailed presentation. You are probably unprepared for the assault! The same principle applies to reports. Familiarize users with a concise snapshot with an executive summary. This introductory section should provide a clear overview of the purpose of the report, key findings, and recommendations.

- Elaborate progressively. Break down your report into short paragraphs in line with the story that you have formulated, making sure to have logical connections between the sections.

- Choose the right elements. In the modern days of "TL;DR", blatantly verbose paragraphs can be annoying and there is a high possibility that such long texts can be ignored. Hence, make use of tables wherever it makes sense, and appropriate visual formats such as graphs to showcase comparisons and trends.

- Keep emotions at bay. When we are talking about reports, it can be anything from presenting an account of facts, experiences, incidents or even email replies. Although your report might be the result of an outburst of emotions in a certain context, make sure not to mix up those emotions in your report, and try to be as neutral and factual as possible.

- Focus on accuracy. Most importantly, make a serious effort to ensure the correctness of the data mentioned in your report, as even a slight error can raise questions about the credibility of the report. Finally, make it a point to proofread your report meticulously to eliminate typos and grammatical errors.

So, next time when you are asked to prepare findings report on an unpleasant incident, empower yourself with the art of storytelling and reporting craftsmanship, and when you express yourself using a combination of the above techniques, you will certainly be perceived the way you had expected to be!

"Good quality stuff is generally not challenged. So, whatever you do should have a class of its own."

31

What's holding you back?

Ever kicked off a new year all pumped and ready to go, just to see as time flies, your big plans stay just as plans? Now, think about your work life, and it's much the same story there. We've all been there, staring down at a deadline, discussing to-dos only to see them ballooning out into an ever-growing list. You have the right intent but probably an inner fear keeps coming up with "logical" reasons and hindering your way forward. This insistence on "just a little later" is nothing but procrastination.

Procrastination is an inner voice that whispers in our ears, convincing us there's always "more time tomorrow." It lives on assumptions – the belief that the task is too difficult, the outcome uncertain, the need for inputs, or the clarity waiting to be given by "someone". Sometimes, it's an inherent habit of staying in a comfort zone, that we find ourselves slipping back into. Or perhaps, it stems from a fear of self-doubt, a voice whispering we're not quite there yet. If you find yourself working on future activities, such as something starting next month, inadvertently ignoring the present state, you can safely conclude that you are a victim of procrastination.

The issue with delaying work is that it traps us in a bad, vicious loop. When we push tasks away, they stick in our mind. This makes us more stressed and anxious, which makes starting even harder. As tasks stack up, our self-belief and work output suffer setbacks. We miss due dates, let down our team, and stop ourselves from reaching our true skill. Procrastination is not always about being lazy. There may be something more to it than what appears. You must carefully analyze and understand the reasons behind your procrastination. Look at yourself neutrally so that you don't convince yourself for the delays. By doing so, you can implement effective strategies and break free from its hold and activate your beast mode.

- Fear of not being perfect. If you run behind perfectionism, there is a great chance that the obsession of flawlessness itself can be a major hurdle in even getting started. "See the big picture", "Break down tasks into tangible outcomes", and work on a prototype. Once you have set your eyes on the big picture, you'll certainly work your way towards the perfect outcome. In the process you'll see that you've already started and not waiting for the perfect start.

- Fear of entering the uncharted waters. When you are faced with new challenges or unfamiliar tasks, it is natural to feel apprehensive about the "unknown" and that can act as a major influence in getting started. You must believe that uncharted territory, in a normal work routine, may simply be your perception of something extraordinary due to lack of knowledge. Hence, just get out of your comfort zone, learn the little extra, and get going.

- Fear of failure. Sometimes you are not sure of the solution and are consumed by the looming thoughts of failure. These thoughts keep pulling you back, and although you start your work, it gets dragged by the negativity. The best thing to do is just dive in with belief in your own capabilities and you'll see things unfolding for good.

Here's something you can do right away and win over procrastination.

- Don't insist on buying time. The more you get, the more you will delay.

- Don't think about what you are going to do next week or next month. Focus on what you must do today and act on it without any further delay.

- Find and tackle the anchor task that is likely to be the prime cause that your emotional mind is hesitant to take up causing the ripple delays.

✔ Be an active participant in the initial tussle between your logical mind and emotional mind, but with a positive mindset and a determination to take up what you're afraid of.

✔ Break down your major objective into smaller tasks, make a checklist and celebrate every small success to keep yourself motivated.

"Your mind is the strongest and weakest unseen in this universe and only you decide it to be so."

32

Learn the art of detachment

Perseverance is an important quality when you set out to achieve something intricate. It is this quality that will eventually take you to the destination despite all the odds. However, it comes with a rider. While dedication is crucial, hanging on to obsessive ideas can be counter-productive at times, especially when the direction itself is wrong. This is because although you might have taken the wrong route, the feeling that you have already spent "so much time" can keep you taking back on the same route.

Persistence is invaluable, but stagnation is detrimental. This is where the art of detachment can step in as a powerful tool. It allows you to step back, reassess your approach, and consider alternative paths. Perhaps, new technology or a fresh perspective could take you to new heights, which might not be possible with the present approach. Detachment is not about abandoning your objectives, but it's about building willingness to let go of obsessive patterns to make way for new methods.

Detachment is about acknowledging that sometimes the best path forward lies in starting afresh. Imagine you are working on software that comes up with recurring bugs. You fix those bugs, and they surface again in different forms. How many times will you fix the same issue? Not only does this irritate users, but it also consumes your energy that can be put up into something more fulfilling. Wouldn't it be prudent to acknowledge that the design itself might be wrong, something that you have been obsessed with? Let go of it and you'll suddenly experience freshness, the freshness to think through unbiased ideas and new approaches, something that your mind had been subconsciously resisting from letting them occur in your thoughts.

Think of a writer who began writing a creative article with a sudden spark of thought but is struggling to go past a threshold for want of a fresh flow. Clinging on desperately to the original concept leads to frustration, as the mind keeps revolving around the same storyline. Detachment allows one to step back, discard the current approach, and open possibilities of a fresh start that can be even more rewarding. We often come across disrupting events in our lives, as our life itself is not a linear journey, and is filled with excitement! Imagine you are working on an important project, and suddenly you hear a cracking noise from your hard drive. As a shiver runs through, you pray in desperation hoping to be it's not what you thought. But indeed, it happens to be that unwelcome event, the dreaded hard disk crash. To make things worse, your backup is pretty much dated. "Had I taken regular backups"; "Had I documented it somewhere"; "Had I been more careful"; You'll probably ponder over all those things that you could "have been done" and there will be a good deal of learning for future. However, in the present you are left with only two options – either immerse yourself in the grief of the loss, or recharge as if nothing happened and set out to rise from the ashes with even more vigor, this time with even better techniques.

Easier said than done, here are a few pointers to help practice detachment as a routine.

✔ Step outside of your comfort zone. We get used to certain practices over a period, and this becomes the comfort zone, one of the limiting factors in the pursuit of peak performance. Getting out of the comfort zone requires a deliberate effort and the result can be greatly rewarding.

✔ Don't be afraid to discard past efforts. If you turn a bottle filled with water upside down, you will notice a hesitation of the water to come out due to trapped air being squeezed. Eventually the water comes out due to scientific reasons. We often encounter such hesitation when it comes to discarding work done on something. So, like the trapped air, why resist and delay the process of eventual acceptance?

✔ Find opportunities in disruption. If something disrupts normal routine, and you know there is no way back, accept the reality, and take this as a fresh opportunity without repenting the loss that anyway cannot be recovered.

✔ Step out of the mental loop. If something isn't working out the way it should, it is better to take a fresh look rather than getting entangled in the vicious cycle of the same old thought process.

✔ Try to break a habit. Breaking a habit requires determination, persistence, and willingness to break free from a routine. For instance, try removing a game from your mobile that you are almost addicted to playing. You'll experience internal resistance, and persisting with the removal will open the doors to the art of detachment.

"A change is all that you seek all the time; you can make little alterations in your own life to completely turn it around."

33

Enter the uncharted waters

Let's say you are working in a group on a project that requires certain "specialized" skills, which you don't possess. How would you react to such a situation? It so happens that you generally end up demarcating a line and splitting roles and responsibilities. You feel safe in the process if Team X will handle the "specialized" activity, and you will handle the inputs to that team and integrate their output.

You are safe only as long as everyone else maintains the same level of ignorance. However, you are always in the "insecure zone", for you never know when Team X will enter your territory.

Let's talk a bit about specialization, and the illusion that we have about specialized activity. I'll put forth a simple example that will make it clear. You must have used Microsoft Word. Did you ever try to find out the total number of options available on the Ribbon? Well, I haven't, because it is overwhelming and probably could be well over five hundred. Given this, do you think anyone would claim to be an absolute expert in Microsoft Word? Still, you might say you don't know how to do a certain thing such as mail merge, and some Person X is good at that. Does this mean that Person X is a specialist? No, because even that person might not be aware of all the options available on the Ribbon. But since he knows a thing or two more than what you know, you declare him to be an expert.

In a normal work routine, when you see people around, you can safely assume that the seemingly proficient ones are just five or ten per cent above the average, with a few exceptions, of course. It's just that you have not taken the extra step to explore. Once you decide to explore the foreign territory, you suddenly realize that it wasn't quite specialized! When you finally venture into uncharted territory, you realize that what seemed specialized was merely a surface-level understanding. This first step elevates you to a level playing field and lays the foundation for a bigger leap to surpass your competition. Do this and in no time, you'll find yourself sailing through comfortably in the uncharted waters, creating a niche for yourself!

Here are a few steps that you can take to enter the uncharted waters:

- Do not get overwhelmed by "love at first sight" of a presentation or demonstration.

- Believe that the presenter has knowledge limited only to the tip of the iceberg.

- Believe that there's much more than what is being shown.

- Embrace curiosity and start learning what you are afraid of.

- Overcome the fear and choose to explore what is not within your current reach.

- Take baby steps and gather some confidence.

- Motivate yourself by attempting a small part of what you feel is the most complex.

- Try to navigate towards the bottom of the iceberg.

"Fear exists only until you experience it."

34
Have patience

The modern world is characterized by the urge for quick results and instant gratification. When challenged with a question, the first action that we think of is "Google", and now "GPT" for even faster results. There's nothing wrong with it, as that's the way it is!

Let's expand this a bit further. When you search for something on Google, how often do you go beyond the second page of the search results? Chances are that you probably click on one of the very first few results, and land up with either accepting the solution you get on the first page or ditching the search term and looking for something else. This approach works for ordinary challenges, but as you scout for a niche, it doesn't augur well, because you'll either not find what you're looking for, or you'll get something half-baked that can be potentially compromising. Finding the right solutions require a good investment in a quality that is now on the verge of extinction – Patience!

Patience demands focus, perseverance, and tolerance. Let's say you have planted a seed with the hope that it will blossom quickly. Howsoever frequently you check for the growth, it will take its own time. You wouldn't pull it out from the soil daily to check on its progress. You can only nurture it with water, sunlight, and a lot of patience. Your efforts, combined with time, will eventually yield the flower you waited for. The same principle applies to our goals. One must put in sincere effort and persist in the right direction. Patience allows our effort to take shape and eventually yield the desired results.

Being patient does not mean waiting endlessly and expecting some magic to unfold. It is rather about having belief in your own effort and the process. It is about understanding that sometimes the most powerful actions are the ones we choose not to take – the impulsive decisions and premature conclusions.

If you look around in your own circle, you will find people saying, "I want to increase my patience", or "I want to increase my tolerance". Patience does not come in the form of a magic pill, and certainly not something that you can develop overnight. It can be developed over a period through an integrated approach, through conscious actions in our daily lives. All that is required is a watchful eye and a lot of tolerance and patience!

Sounds confusing? Here's something you can try to gradually increase your patience.

- Explain intricate concepts and designs to interns. Taking some time out to patiently explain concepts to them until they fully grasp it can be a great exercise in patience. Persist with your efforts even if you find yourself "frustrated" due to the huge gap between your experience and their level of understanding.

- Go beyond the third page of search results. If you are not finding what you are looking for on Google, try to scroll through at least five or six pages for your search term. If you did not find anything on the first page, it does not mean that you won't get a clue somewhere in the deep. Go on patiently and you will find something hidden!

- Be a keen listener. When you work in a team, you are bound to experience some unpleasant communication. At times, there will be an emotional outburst from your team members. Listen with empathy even if you know that only 20% of this communication is objective. The remaining 80% is towards building your own patience! This is irrespective of what level you assume in the corporate ladder.

- Experiment in the kitchen. Cooking delicious food takes time. If something must simmer, it must be allowed to simmer and not cooked on high flame out of impatience. Do this compulsive exercise and it will be a great lesson in patience.

✓ Try not to blow the horn. Have you observed fellow bikers when you are waiting at the traffic signal? There is only a split second of gap between the signal turning green and you getting forced to move by incessant honking. That's impatience at its peak! So, if you are also in the habit of honking at the traffic signal, simply try to avoid it and wait for your turn. Trust the process and go with the flow. This everyday life habit can drastically improve your patience at the subconscious level.

Wait for the right opportunity to overtake. You may be a skilled driver and always keen to get ahead of other vehicles. Chances are that in this process you may be putting yourself at risk through dangerous overtaking. Sometimes you may find yourself admitting to yourself that it was a "narrow escape". Instead, stay calm and wait for the perfect moment to overtake. This life habit will not only make your journeys safe but will also greatly help in cultivating patience!

"Embrace every situation as an opportunity to learn something new and exciting that you wouldn't experience otherwise."

35

Give examples that connect

Illustrations play a crucial role in communication. When used in the right context, they have the potential to evoke strong emotions such as excitement, fear, anger, inspiration, and vigor, prompting the desired actions from the other person. For instance, if you are working on a project that's tight on schedule and you want to get the job done anyhow, you'll have to work on stirring the emotion of inspiration to get your team charged up; while if you are presenting a new feature idea for a product, you'll have to work on generating excitement for the product manager. The right example can transform dry information into a captivating story, a spark that ignites understanding and action.

Imagine trying to explain the concept of virtual reality to someone who has never experienced it. You may try to explain in theoretical terms how virtual reality immerses you in a digital world, allowing you to interact with objects and environments as if they were real. Chances are, this might still fall flat even with the use of power words such as "exhilarating experience", "3D", "epic", because the connection is not established. But the moment you picture an experience such as, "Imagine you're cooking something, and you get two additional hands on either side, each one holding your real hand turn by turn and helping you to cook the best recipe of your life!". You've just roused an emotion!

Examples are important because human tendency is such that it is driven by comparisons. We are naturally inclined to make comparisons. We instinctively assess examples in the context of our own experiences, knowledge, and beliefs. Comparing things helps us grasp new ideas better and assess what might happen as a result. By providing relatable examples, you tap into this tendency, making it easier for people to easily understand your point of view and quickly get them on your side.

Here's how you can go about illustrating your point of view and invoke the desired actions:

✔ Don't just inform, inspire! Think about how you want your listeners to feel – passionate, motivated, empowered. Build your story in a way such that it connects with the listeners and stirs the same emotions.

✔ Sometimes, ordinary examples might not leave the desired impact you're aiming for. In such cases using extreme situations can better drive your objective. For example, when talking about software performance, comparing it to the precision required for a rocket launcher can emphasize the importance of reliability and accuracy. But be careful while choosing the boundaries because examples that are out of context will still be worthless.

✔ The best examples are those that resonate with your audience. Draw from their world, their experiences, to create a connection that sparks understanding and action.

✔ Sometimes, you may have to give seemingly impossible examples, as a little shock can be effective as well. Talking about achieving a full middle split for someone quite inflexible in two weeks might seem extreme, but it perfectly illustrates the importance of committing oneself to achieve extraordinary results.

✔ Have you ever heard of "boundary value testing" in computer parlance? The idea is that a well-written code generally works in normal circumstances, but the chances of failure are greater on the borderline values. The same goes for examples. Ordinary examples may be seen as run-of-the-mill and of not much significance, but the ones right at the boundary of "what-if" have a greater chance of establishing the desired connection.

"Stay conscious and logical at all times; it is very easy for your mind to believe in something that never was."

36
Learn the art of expectation management

Before we start talking about how to handle expectations well, let's understand why it's so important. Whether it's at work or in your personal life, managing expectations is vastly important for things to go well. Imagine a world where things are always changing, and you're not sure what's going to happen next. That's when managing expectations becomes important. It can make the difference between things going great and being disappointed. Whether you're leading a group, dealing with customers, or just talking to friends, knowing what everyone expects is the key. Managing expectations isn't just about doing what people want. It's also about making sure everyone understands what's going on and avoids any surprises.

Expectation management is an art because:

- It involves a delicate balance of understanding, communication, and adaptation. Like any form of art, it requires skill, intuition, and creativity.
- It deals with deep understanding of desires, motives, and perspectives of all involved parties. This requires empathy, intuition, and the ability to see beyond surface-level expectations to grasp underlying needs and concerns.
- It involves conveying complex ideas clearly and persuasively.
- It demands flexibility and adaptability, adjusting your approach to accommodate changing circumstances, diverse personalities, and evolving expectations.
- It deals with achieving harmony and alignment in tight situations involving competing priorities, conflicting interests, and limited resources.

If your boss prefers certain colors, and you disagree in the context of the project, it's best not to argue excessively as it could lead to unnecessary tension. Instead, consider creating two designs with different color combinations, even if that means putting in extra time and energy: one that aligns with the preferences of your boss and another that reflects your own design principles. Present both options with clear reasoning, showing your willingness to accommodate their preferences while also advocating your own perspective. This approach demonstrates effective expectation management and persuasive communication without sounding negative. By adopting this simple exercise, you are incorporating key elements of the art of expectation management listed above, including understanding, communication, adaptation, creativity, and balance.

Here's how you can accommodate expectation management in your routine:

- Understand your audience, their strengths, weaknesses, likes and dislikes.

- Finish your draft (whether it's a design, document, letter, sitemap, or anything else), and promptly integrate their preferences while removing any aspects they don't like.

- If you are writing a letter or preparing a presentation on behalf of someone, it's crucial not to use your own language or style. Instead, put yourself in the shoes of the individual on whose behalf you are writing and tailor your language to reflect their tone and perspective.

- At times, you must do it against your mind, but then it's a matter of perception management and enhancing your performance.

"You can win by not defeating others, but by winning them over through your good actions."

37

Don't miss that thing

I'll keep coming back to perspectives and perceptions because success is a relative term. The more perfect you are, the more minutely you will be observed. You may put in your 100 per cent, yet you may still be short by 99 per cent. That's harsh, but I'm sure you must have at some point come across such an irony. A popular satire in medical field, "the operation was successful, but the patient died", is a perfect example of relativity of success.

As I said, success is a relative term, and so is quality. Let's say, you are part of a ten-member team. Nine of them are terribly poor in English writing and you happen to be an excellent writer. Now, suppose one fine day your manager asks you all to pen down thoughts on a certain concept that he has come up with. The nine people in your team submit their documents and so do you. Your manager reads through their text and appreciates the good ones, although those were written in broken English. To your astonishment, your manager points out that you have missed a comma in one of the sentences. Just imagine the amount of frustration that would take your mind in a fraction of a second, because you had witnessed how the others were appreciated despite their pathetic writing, and your trivial grammatical error got highlighted. This is what I mean by 'that' thing. Once again, the more perfect you are, the more minutely you will be observed. A tailender batsman will be recognized for a short cameo of 20 or 30 runs and will always overshadow a top order batsman falling short of a century by one run.

The point is, you must be vigilant enough to not allow something trivial to overshadow and ruin the effort that you have put in towards making the 'real' thing.

Here's a simple checklist that will help:

- Make a list of all the finer level points that you must cover as part of the project.

- Complete your work and keep it as a draft.

- Run through your draft as a critic in an unbiased manner and verify with the list you created in the first step.

- Pay special attention to the specific demands of your internal audience.

- Make sure you have not left anything unattended, such as missing pin code in an address, or keeping the website title as "Just another WordPress site", or naming your document as "Document1.docx", and there are plenty such silly things that we keep doing.

- Understand your internal audience; pump in extra effort to incorporate their weak points (language, grammar, colors, fonts, taglines, buzzwords, and so on).

- Remember that if you are given a super white blank paper with a small black dot somewhere, it is the black dot that gets the attention and not the super white charm of the paper. Treat your work as white paper and make a conscious effort to identify the black spot.

"You must work exceptionally hard for the insignificant 1% that can potentially overshadow the relentless effort put behind the exceptional 99%."

38

Begin where the strongest ends

Have you ever observed how projects are paced in the initial phases? There is excitement, every day something is being produced, and everyone is full of energy. However, as time passes by and the project starts stabilizing in a routine mode, things start slowing down. That's obvious though, as you cannot expect something tangible to be "created" every now and then. It is at this point that people tend to give up, looking out for alternatives in the pretext of "no opportunity" although the big picture may still be miles away from completion.

Now consider a second scenario. In complex projects involving technological research you may experience sprints of intermediate breakthroughs, followed by harrowing silence as nothing tangible seems to be coming out. Even some of the brightest minds are consumed by self-doubt in this silence, and this is the point where many tend to give up, demoralized.

Both these scenarios are characterized by the tendency of "giving up a bit too early". You may not be far away from the destination, yet due to the invisible nature of the path, you may not want to drift any further, and hence give up.

However, there is a way to remain tuned, and the fruits are truly deserving. The trick lies in persevering through uncertainty and preserving your energy. Imagine yourself running a marathon. Would you expect yourself to sprint the entire marathon at a constant pace? Certainly not. You would keep running at different speeds, change your grip, recharge yourself by engaging in healthy distractions, refresh your mind and spirit by motivating yourself with affirmations such as "don't give up yet", and "just a little more". While this example pertains to physical activity, it is the underlying mental strength that fuels this energy, and hence relevant.

When you are working in a team, you'll be surrounded by people who would be at par with you, some less proficient than you, while some more talented than you. In order to make a mark, you must thrive until your goals are met, and here are some ways that you can gain momentum when most others give up.

- Compartmentalize tasks making sure that you'll get a taste of success in each compartment.

- Celebrate the small victories, and the milestones achieved. Each step forward becomes your fuel, propelling you past self-doubt and fatigue.

- Keep invoking your grit, determination, and the knowledge that true strength lies in pushing beyond perceived limits.

- Motivation is a powerful tool, and recognizing your progress keeps the fire burning brighter than most of the others.

- Feel the energy when you recognize that you have risen from a point where others have given up.

- Visualize yourself crossing the finish line, not because you were the fastest, but because you had the endurance to go the distance.

- Keep affirming yourself as being capable of surpassing even the "strongest" – all it takes is the will to begin where they end.

"Preserve some energy… Activate it when everyone else is exhausted."

39

Identify your turning point

In our daily lives, we come across many opportunities to make a positive impact on ourselves. When seized wisely, these opportunities can become crucial turning points in different areas of our lives, including career, academics, sports, and more.

You might have witnessed someone going from being an underdog to a standout success, and pondered on what made this remarkable transformation. In most cases, the key lies in their awareness of the situation and sharp presence of mind. A person who was once unknown suddenly becomes a star, and that marks it as a significant turning point.

Turning point isn't just a lucky break, but a conscious effort to engage with an opportunity and utilize your skills to achieve great outcomes. Take a moment to ponder over the opportunities that you might have missed.

Here's a story for your inspiration. Once there was a three-day workshop on Business Communication. The speaker, with his eloquent command over English, had already mesmerized the students, most of which were from lower divisions in the school, known to be those with failures and low scorers. The students became very comfortable within just a few minutes and were more than willing to answer the questions the speaker would pose. Continuing the context of the topic, he suddenly asked the class to raise hands if anyone was able to list five words starting with the letter "A". Barring a few shy ones, almost the entire class asserted. When he randomly asked a handful of students, they were rightly able to tell their words that started with A. It was a simple exercise! The session continued the next day. After narrating a few stories and case studies, this time he requested the class to raise their hands if anyone could list five words starting with the letter K. Now, this was unexpected. Yet some of the students, a very few though, were able to list KNOCK, KNACK, KNOWLEDGE, KNOWN, KNIT, KICK, KILO, KEEP, and so on, but there was a visible discomfort in recalling these words. It was now the last day of the workshop, and the speaker was keen on delivering a lifelong learning message to the students and had something already cooked up in his mind. Towards the end of the session, the speaker asked the class, "Now class, please raise your hands if anyone can list five words starting with the letter… umm… 'X'". Unsurprisingly, there were no takers for this question. The speaker simplified it further and reduced the number 4…3…2. Yes, for two, the entire class knew it was X-MAS and X-RAY. When there were no more, and the speaker was about to deliver his closing punch, a boy sitting on the last bench raised his hand and asked for permission to list five words. He then began… XYLEM, XENOPHONE, XENOPHOBIA, XEBEC, XYSTER. A wave of astonishment swept through the entire class as every head swiveled towards him in utter disbelief. The speaker was equally stunned, and asked the boy if he knew the meaning of any of these words. This boy had done his homework well, and he could explain all these words. He didn't stop there. He listed another three words!

This entire episode was such impactful that within a few minutes the entire school was looking up to this boy in admiration, oblivious of the fact that he belonged to a lower division and without a glorious academic record. That was his turning point, and there was no turning back.

Among the large group, there was this one boy who had sensed an opportunity; an opportunity to stand out and make a mark, an opportunity to distinguish himself from the rest, an opportunity to make his presence known with vigor. He had done his homework and executed it with perfection.

Probably it was his luck, his day, you'd argue. Agreed. But opportunity knocks just like that, and each opportunity doesn't materialize the way it should be. The important point to note is that this boy sensed and prepared for the same intelligently.

Each passing day hands us numerous opportunities. Take a moment to look back and find all those turning points, small or big, in your life, cherish those moments, celebrate, and recharge yourself. You must remain alert and grab them with both hands. Here are some choices that you can make in daily life to transform otherwise routine situations into turning points of your life.

These points are elaborated elsewhere in this book.

- See the big picture.
- Find yourself in the corner.
- Someone must do the actual work, you be that.
- Identify your leadership spot.
- Be uncomfortable.
- Spring a surprise.
- Enter the uncharted waters.
- Begin where the strongest ends.

"You just have one moment to seize before it becomes a lost opportunity."

40

There is always a room to accommodate

You might have often come across the feeling of being trapped by the limits of time and resources. There's so much to do but you just don't have the time. In a relatable scenario, when you are working on a project, especially the one that is in the process of progressive evolution, and new requirements keep piling up, you might get the feeling of being pushed into the corner, and there's an inner voice that screams, "I don't have room to accommodate!".

It is true that we all have finite time and capabilities. As a general tendency, our instant reaction is, "There's no way I can fit this in" and thus we shut down the possibility of exploring creative solutions. But have you ever questioned yourself? Is this imaginary, your own perception of the self-imposed boundaries? Is this an illusion that can be decoded? Can you exploit your full potential by not shrinking ambitions, but by expanding perspectives?

The truth is, our greatest enemy lives within us, our own subconscious mind that influences the first response to a situation. Sometimes we are prompted to automatically say **"No"** to new ideas. Reason? We feel overwhelmed or are limited by our existing commitments. But often, this **"No"** is due to the fear of stepping outside our comfort zone or a lack of belief in our own abilities. When our first response begins with "**No**", we limit ourselves. On the other hand, when our first response is "**Yes**", we begin on an affirmative note, and this can travel a long distance towards a positive outcome.

Further, what follows the **Yes** or **No** has its own significance. Let's say for instance, you are working on a project, on a neck-to-neck schedule, and your boss comes to you and says, "The product has come up good. But we need to incorporate this new feature that is going to make it a massive hit in the market". In such a situation, since you are aware of the time and resources at your disposal, you may come up with any of these response variations:

- A plain "**No, I can't accommodate it**" – Complete denial, and no way to move forward. Here you close the doors for any further discussion, and since you have your mind closed, the requested feature, in most probability, is not going to be a part of the product in the current schedule.

- "**No, but…**" – Denial, but with a bleak chance of considering. For example,

- "**No, but how am I going to fit this within the schedule**" – You may be open to advice on how to manage your resources optimally.

- "**No, but why would anyone want to…**" – You may be open to discussing the idea.

- "**No, but when do you want it to…**" – You may be willing to take it up but in the next sprint.

- "**Yes, but…**" – You are convinced, but unsure how to go about doing it. This is a positive variation of "No, but…", and hence has a better chance of receiving the idea with an open mindset.

- "**Yes, and…**" – This simple shift in mindset opens the door to accommodation and innovation. It allows you to acknowledge the challenge ("Yes, this sounds exciting") while simultaneously acknowledging your capacity to find a solution ("And, I'm resourceful and capable of figuring it out").

Try to relate this with your most recent project. You'll certainly find something similar that must have happened. Remember to do this very exercise with a "**Yes, and…**" approach and you'll find interesting insights for your own!

So, the next time, when you are saying "**No**", just remind yourself that it could be something that you can possibly accommodate, just with a few affirmations in the "**Yes, and…**" approach.

Here are some:

- You can accommodate new requests in your schedule just by streamlining processes.
- You have immense capability, just believe in yourself.
- You have unlimited potential.
- You have infinite capacity.
- Exploit the complete possibility of "Yes" before you say "No".

"Be present and deliberate in your choices as your life is shaped by the choices you make."

41

Treat everything as primary activity

Have you ever felt a pull towards an activity, something you knew you would enjoy, but haven't pursued? Imagine aspirations beyond work, like learning a new language, writing a book, mastering a skill, or just focusing on yourself. Have you ever had goals like those that haven't come to fruition? We are referring to activities not imposed by your professional obligations, but rather those you considered trying your hand at.

Here are a few examples to spark your thoughts:

- You wanted to learn a musical instrument, but you don't have a musical background.
- You wanted to learn a programming language, but that's outside of your current niche.
- You wanted to study a field of science or technology, but that's outside of your expertise.
- You wanted to learn a new language, such as Spanish or Japanese, but just as a hobby.
- You wanted to achieve a full split, but you are not a gymnast.
- You wanted to become a blogger, but you are short of time.

Most of us fail to experience a shift in the above verb tense, such as transformation of "You wanted to learn" into "You learnt", or "You wanted to study" into "You studied". Don't worry, you're not alone. The distinction between core activities and "extras" is interesting, and it affects how we prioritize our time and energy. We often prioritize essential tasks, leaving these personal explorations as "extracurricular", especially when we are juggling busy schedules.

Getting your aspirations materialized isn't too difficult though!

The key is to carve out intentional space for these activities, treating them as priorities alongside other commitments. Schedule these pursuits like you would for important meetings, making them non-negotiable parts of your calendar. If you are wondering, how would you find time from your busy schedule, then the solution lies in "compartmentalizing". You must create a separate mental compartment, that will have a dedicated time slot and your complete attention. How much time you take out is not important initially, like a flowing stream, it will figure out on its own as you progress.

So, now it's time to pursue what you always wanted to. Start today, as the wait for the "right time" would be infinite. Here's how you can go about achieving your goals that are not in your mainstream routine:

- Make a firm resolve to pursue your passion.

- Start living your passion by imagining yourself immersed in it.

- Take out one hour for this activity.

- Compartmentalize it such that you are completely involved physically and mentally.

- Treat this as a primary activity, and not as an "addon" activity. The moment you label something as an addon activity, you inadvertently persuade yourself that it's optional and not a mandatory commitment.

I <u>wanted to</u> write this book, and being an "extra", over the years it gathered dust just as an "aspiration". It gained momentum and took shape only when I started treating this as a primary activity having its own compartment that automatically found space without affecting my routine schedule.

"All thoughts remain on paper if they are not put into practice, and the best time to start implementing them is now."

42
Strive for longevity

It is always our wish to be the best at whatever we do whether it is in the office, hobby or even sports. Nevertheless, being at your best does not come and go like a flash of brilliance followed by long silences. It has to do with being good for years by struggle and consistency; that's what really matters. What makes people continue this journey? Perseverance, persistence, and longevity.

This means prioritizing practices and behaviors that lead to success over time in relation to work life, habits, and overall performance. It also involves cultivating habits which promote personal growth as well as development of professionalism instead of seeking temporal solutions through quick fixes.

For instance, consider day traders who take a position in stocks just for a day versus long term investors. To make money from short term price changes, intraday traders buy and sell stocks rapidly within a single trading day. Nonetheless, because the market is unpredictable, while some may earn huge amounts of money, most will incur tremendous losses. On the other hand, there are others like Warren Buffet who prefer long-term investment strategies rather than quick cash through stock markets such as intraday trading. It is for a good reason that he is among the richest people on earth!

By adopting a long-term mindset and consistently investing in actions that promote resilience, adaptability, and continuous improvement, you are all set for long-term success.

Here's how you can practice longevity:

- Envision what you set out to achieve.

- Immerse yourself in the imagination of your vision.

- Commit yourself to reach out to your vision despite all the obstacles.

- Keep finding alternate solutions to reach your goal.

- Maintain faith in your ability to achieve your goals, regardless of challenges.

- Persevere through adversity, refusing to prematurely abandon your aspirations.

- Acknowledge and celebrate each milestone achieved on your journey, fueling your determination as you progress.

- Commit to perform an activity daily, for example writing "श्री राम जय राम जय जय राम" eleven times in a diary and make it a point to do this without fail.

A simple exercise like this will help you to build consistency over a long period of time.

"You shall not be defeated unless you choose to."

43

Learn the art of compartmentalizing

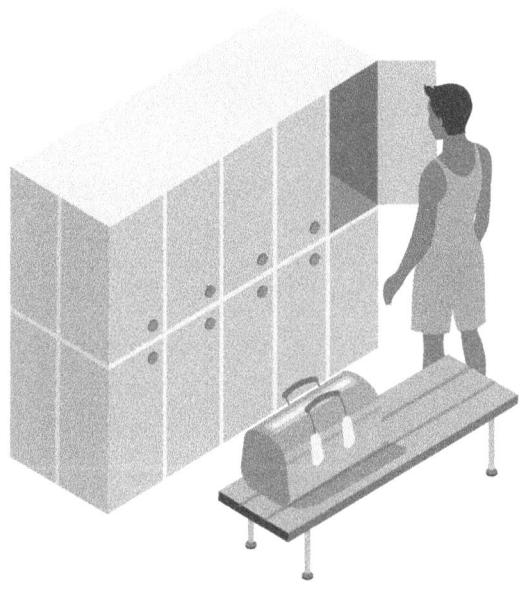

Love, humor, wonder, courage, calmness, anger, sadness, fear, and disgust - These are nine fundamental emotions, known as the NAVARASA in Hindu philosophy. One of these emotions, or a variation of these, is triggered for every event that you participate in either directly or indirectly. Thus, our mind shuffles between these emotions throughout the day; sometimes we are aware while most of the time we tend to forget the present moment. Each emotion has its own unique value. But an uncontrolled mashup of these emotions can cause havoc in our daily routine. As we respond to a given situation as per our present state of mind, a mix-up of emotions can have a direct impact on our performance. Thus, if you are sitting in a meeting with your colleagues, and suddenly you happen to engage in a heated discussion with a vendor, and you come back to the meeting with that angry mindset, I leave the outcome of the meeting with your colleagues to your own imagination!

This is where compartmentalization steps in. It allows each situation to have its own designated space. Compartmentalization is not about locking down emotions, but it is about developing the ability to acknowledge and process emotions without letting them hijack your focus on the activity in hand. You can do this easily by allowing your emotions to be processed in isolation. Attend to the situation, consciously pick the objective outcomes, and return sans the emotions! By mastering the technique of processing emotions in separate compartments, you ensure that external factors do not affect one activity while engaging in another.

Managing emotions through compartmentalization isn't as intimidating as it appears at first glance. In fact, it bears great resemblance to how we manage physical exertion. While running a marathon, you don't sprint from start to finish without taking a break, but you pace yourself. You need strategic rest so that your body can regulate its temperature, refill energy, and adapt to the pace requirements of the run. Just like neglecting rest during a marathon can lead to exhaustion, ignoring "emotional breaks" can lead to a tangled web of thoughts leading to frustration and ultimately, depression.

Here's how you can practice compartmentalization:

✔ Maintain a work-life differentiation. Set up your own routines such that they mark transitions between different aspects of your life. For instance, when you play a sport, you set up yourself in the attire of that sport. Similarly, when you switch from work to personal life, simply switch to a comfortable attire and this can work as a trigger for your mind to switch to relax mode. Devise your own routines and see the difference it makes!

✔ Practice separating emotions from one another. Try to focus on the active task, leaving aside worries of the other. When you switch between topics or tasks, make sure to close the previous one before starting the next. Avoid the temptation to multitask and keep your focus solely on the current task at hand.

✔ Listen to your favorite music track during your commute back home. Enjoy the journey even if it is marred with traffic. You may already know there's something unpleasant waiting for you at home. But that's after you reach home. So, until then, free yourself for the duration of your journey and let your mind immerse itself in the rhythm of the music. Whatever is going to happen at home, let it take its own course. You cannot change that by worrying in advance. Enjoy this travel time and recharge yourself for the upcoming challenge.

✔ Leave work-related frustrations at the office. Try to cross the exit door of your office consciously and not unknowingly. When you cross the door, take a moment to pause at the door, and visualize dropping all the work-related emotions, and switch to your personal identity. Carrying negative emotions home can lead to an imbalance between work and personal life. While you may work from home, leave the associated emotions behind.

✔ Similarly, when leaving for work, let go of any worries or concerns. Creating a clear boundary between work and personal life can help maintain a healthy balance.

✔ Engage yourself in some sport, preferably a group sport such as Badminton, or Tennis, that will help create a compartment consisting of a team that is different from your daily routine.

"It's all in the mind."

44

Get everyone on a common page

When you have the option to work as an individual contributor, you have a greater chance of performing optimally by utilizing your own expertise, tools, and techniques. However, in a corporate environment, you will find yourself working with teams more often than the freedom to work individually. The moment you step into a team, as a member, leader, or manager, you can safely assume that your performance is at stake; not because of your inability, but because everyone may not be on a common page. In any collaborative endeavor, everyone needs to be on a common page for a successful outcome.

Here's a seemingly trivial example of how a small mix-up can possibly lead to the collapse of an entire project. Suppose you are a working on a photo shooting project that involves shooting two different types of photos of a thousand people – cover photos in a candid pose, and candid photos. Your team is a cross-functional one, consisting of developers that are building a platform for managing the photo inventory, the photographers who are clicking the photos and recording the metadata, the graphics team that is dealing with the artwork and printing, the third-party printing agency, and the customer itself. Now imagine the chaos if the photographers were to mix-up the meaning of "candid photos" and "photos with candid pose". A small misunderstanding like this one can change the entire outcome, and considering thousands of photos, the project is guaranteed to take a beating.

Individually each one in the team might be brilliant but just because the directions, jargon, and processes are different, you may find yourself struggling. This is the crux of getting everyone on a common page and aligning everyone on a common platform towards a single objective. Here are some pointers that will help bring everyone together on a common page.

✔ Get everyone to speak the same language. Ensure everyone involved in the project uses the same terminology, even if it means adopting specific jargon or acronyms. This eliminates confusion, establishes clarity in communication, and ensures everyone is on the same wavelength.

✔ Follow unified terminology. While striving for a common language, sometimes even "wrong" terms become universally understood within a project. If a specific term, although technically inaccurate, is consistently used and understood by everyone, it might be more efficient to adopt it within the project for the sake of clarity.

✔ Scan documents carefully. In today's digital age, sharing information often involves scanning documents using the mobile camera. Let's consider a scenario of a project for which you have requested your remote team members to send you a status report of work done for the day in the form of specific data points, which you intend to update in an app later. Picture this: four team members send you their work reports, each spanning five pages, scanned differently – some in portrait and some in landscape orientation. Naturally, reading and processing data in portrait orientation is much easier than constantly tilting your neck to read each line, right? Therefore, establish a protocol for data sharing in advance, and witness how much time you can save!

✔ Agree on common design philosophy. Consider a seemingly trivial example of an application that has a couple of data entry screens, distributed among a couple of developers. Imagine each developer captioning the action button differently, such as, "Submit", "Save", "Post", "Let's Go", and so on. Get everyone on a common page! Establish a consistent naming convention, whether right or wrong is a different story, but agree on a common terminology for the sake of consistency.

✔ Agree on the scope of work. If you do not maintain proper communication and consent of all stakeholders, irrespective of how hard you work, all your effort can be wasted in the form of missed deadlines, budget overruns, and ultimately, project failure. Hence, take deliberate effort to finalize the scope and let it be known and agreed upon.

✔ Set realistic expectations. Get all stakeholders to know about the operating constraints. Be transparent about the resources available, potential constraints, and set realistic deadlines. This helps set achievable expectations and prevents frustration going forward.

The above is just a glimpse of some tweaks that you can make in your routine and ramp up your performance without delving into anything extraordinary! Be mindful of the irritations that you face, and you will automatically figure out those points where you need to get everyone on a common page.

"You see the world as you perceive it to be, see it wisely because perceptions are real as their consequences are real."

45

Find your "It all began with…" moment

Do you find yourself in awe when you read or hear a success story? We often see the triumphant end, the trophy raised, and the booming business. Success stories are always inspiring, and often leave us wondering, "where did they even begin?". There's so much that goes on achieving what we see as great success. Ask any successful person, and they will have a story to tell. Their story is not one that with starts with the present victory post, but one that goes like, "It all began with…".

"It all began with…" are powerful words having great significance. Take Dr. Vijay Bhatkar, the Father of Indian Supercomputing, for instance. He didn't magically wake up one day with the blueprint of PARAM Supercomputer in hand. "It all began with" India's request to USA for a Supercomputer, which was denied. That denial became the spark that ignited his passion, leading him to build India's own Supercomputer.

Or consider Mr. Ratan Tata. His acquisition of Jaguar Land Rover didn't start with a pleasant handshake and a simple exchange of the JLR logo. "It all began with" a challenge, a moment of humiliation when in the year 1998, Mr. Ford said TATA doesn't know how to make cars, and they should stay away from the cars segment. This humiliation became the driving force that led to TATA eventually acquiring JLR, and that too at a massive discount!

Look closely and you will find that the starting point of greatness can be anything but glamorous. It can be a failure, a setback, a challenge, humiliation, or a discomfort. It's the opportunity that knocks in different forms, and it's up to you to seize and build on top of it. Read more about countering such situations in "Find yourself in the corner". Look for your starting point. It could be as trivial as the dissatisfaction you feel with your current routine, a challenge you have been avoiding, or a passion waiting to be reactivated. Most often, we look back in hindsight, and connect the dots after the fact. It doesn't have to be so. Your own "it all began with…" moment might be right in front of you. Identify that trigger and engage yourself in writing your own story, rather than looking back in retrospection.

Travel back in time right now and try to find your "it all began with…" moments. Think about a hobby idea that you pursued, a skill that you acquired, a course that you took, a project that you delivered, or anything that you feel is worth your attention. You don't need any dramatic event to be your "it all began with…" moment. This very book, in fact, originated from a handful of scribbled one-liner notes that I used to write to motivate my team. A simple act of acknowledging that "beginning" was all that was needed, followed by a passion towards fulfilling it.

So, take a moment to pause, and reflect, and recognize your starting point. Find your spark, your "it all began with…" moment, that is waiting to be written in your own story of peak performance.

46

Be uncomfortable

Throughout this book, we have written about ways of finding comfort. We've talked about creating performance enhancement routines, establishing healthy habits, and engaging yourself for maintaining peace of mind. But now we're asking you to be uncomfortable. Yes, you read that right. Discomfort is the feeling that can be your greatest ally on the path of peak performance.

You may feel safe in your comfort zone, but remember that it is the most insecure position to be in. Comfort zones are breeding grounds for stagnation. While it gives a cozy feeling in the familiar environment, it comes at the cost of innovation. Comfortable position means there is no starvation, and as we know, "starvation is the mother of creativity". Thus, when you choose to remain in the comfort zone, you are not doing anything out of the box, and just thriving on the routine. Innovation, on the other hand, lives on pushing boundaries, on venturing into the unknown, the "uncharted waters".

Our mind is a powerhouse. It has limitless potential. Our limits are often self-imposed. Think out of your comfort zone and push yourself beyond these boundaries. It's like any other muscle – it needs to be challenged and stretched to become stronger. When you try to stretch a muscle, you feel the pain, and there's the tussle between your logical mind and emotional mind. Sometimes you persist but most of the time you give up! The outcome is truly rewarding If you step out of the comfort zone and persist through the momentary pain.

In a routine work life, it is important to recognize the discomfort within comfort. Sometimes we get so used to a routine that we start believing it the way it is. Let's say, you are working on a Microsoft Word document created by a colleague. It is a poorly formatted document, with plenty of spaces instead of tabs, "illusionary" page breaks inserted using multiple ENTER keystrokes and not Ctrl + ENTER, no use of heading styles, bullets, and so on. The comfort here is that something has been created and you just follow the template using copy/paste. Recognize the discomfort!

- The page alignment changes each time you hit the ENTER KEY.

- You are unable to maintain the consistency of heading style and numbering automatically.

- Tabs must be aligned manually.

- You must apply fonts and styles each time you insert new content.

You can open possibilities for improvement only if you acknowledge the above discomfort. That's the gist of being uncomfortable.
Try to find discomfort in your routine work. Here are a few techniques that will help you recognize discomfort and win over it:

- Keep an eye on repetitive complaints from your clients, colleagues, or friends. Work on root cause analysis if you find such patterns.

- An opportunity to lead a team or deliver a speech can make you feel nervous. Take this opportunity head-on to make a mark.

- Acknowledge the irritation if you find yourself engaged in too laborious an activity in Excel. This can be your gateway to exploring formulas, macros, or data analysis using AI.

- Feel uncomfortable when your manager points out the same mistake in your work repeatedly. Acknowledge that there is a problem and work towards overcoming it permanently.

- Being on a communication platform such as WhatsApp isn't optional anymore. However, being in countless groups, and quitting those being non-negotiable for social reasons, can be greatly counter-productive. Consider muting such groups for a distraction free work routine!

The above is just a glimpse of how you can fish out all that which you find seemingly comfortable in a routine but are great productivity bottlenecks. Find your own reasons to be uncomfortable, acknowledge those, get irritated, feel starved and then march towards peak performance using creative techniques.

Being uncomfortable does not mean recklessly throwing yourself into chaos. It's rather about making conscious choices to challenge the status quo. It's about acknowledging your fears and then taking that courageous step forward.

47

Find yourself in wondrous amazement

Have you seen how kids are full of curiosity? During their early years of learning, everything new that they see lights up their eyes in amusement. Such is their thirst for curiosity, that they keep churning questions tirelessly. Curiosity is the spark that gives birth to amazing creations. However, as we grow into adulthood, that spark often dims down. We get excessively consumed by our routine and responsibilities. Our "logical mind" takes control and plays the role of the ever-present inner critic. We tend to ignore amusement and instead engage our mind in criticizing and finding the underlying logic.

"Adbhuta", or "wondrous amazement" is one of the nine emotions that is at the core in the journey of innovation. It is the force that pushes our desire to explore, discover, and understand the world around us. When astonishment goes missing, you are always at the risk of finding yourself dragged into the status quo. It is an inner signal of stagnation that compels you to accept things as they are, and once you start doing so, it means you have pretty much settled yourself down in the mundane routine. Are you going to find any excitement in a set routine? Probably not. And, if you are devoid of excitement, there is little motivation to step up. It's a vicious cycle!

The reasons for amazement don't have to be limited to marvels or miracles only. Our everyday observations present us with numerous such opportunities. For example, there are two ways to react when you see a colleague automating a tedious task for you, saving hours with clever Excel macros, and helping to complete your work fast - One, you feel relieved and leave home early, or second, you are greatly amazed and are curious to learn the technique. Look around and you'll find something astonishing that you had ignored for so long!
Rewind your day and ask yourself for one thing that amused you today. Introspect carefully and I'm sure you'll find at least one such

So, find a reason to be amazed! Here's how you can apply amazement in a routine work life:

- Avoid getting into the logic trap instantly. When you see something astonishing, let your inner self express its amusement. If you begin with "Ah! It's simple, nothing great, I know how it's done!", you inadvertently put an instant barrier on further exploration.

- We all use smartphones these days. Do you know which version of the operating system you are on? Invoke curiosity, try to find out if your phone supports the latest version! It's not greed, but the urge to feel the craving.

- Get amazed by the advances in artificial intelligence, robotics, internet of things, augmented and virtual reality, and upgrade yourself to the latest and emerging trends in your field of work.

- Appreciate the work done by someone. By truly marveling at someone's expertise, you delve deeper into the "how" of their work, and that gets you into the upgrade mode.

- The next time you order something online, allow yourself to be amused by the dedication of the delivery person who fought the scorching summer heat or weathered the pouring rain and navigated the streets against all odds to honor your delivery.

- Amazement is viral. Just share and it creates a ripple effect. It opens threads about new ideas and encourages others to contribute their bit. This is one important technique to get everyone to think about potential solutions to complex problems.

Your wondrous amazement shouldn't remain a fantasy forever. It could be a magic trick, a technical tip, or a form of art. Try to uncover the secret once you are amazed by it, and scout for another one! Find avenues to implement the acquired secret, if it falls within the purview of your work, and experience a massive performance boost.

"Wondrous amazement lights up the spark within you to truly explore the infinite potential of your imagination and creativity."

48

Your best is yet to come

You may have accomplished many noteworthy feats in the past, and it is common to dwell on those events. Remembering what you did before can be very helpful when it comes to inspiring yourself. Read "Motivate yourself", in which I have mentioned "look back to look ahead" as a strategy for self-motivation. But if you find yourself frequently citing examples of your greatest accomplishments from years ago, it might indicate that your current development has hit a snag.

When you rely a little too much on past glories, it can be a sign that you are no longer pushing yourself to achieve new heights or take on fresh challenges. You have countered challenges successfully before. You have achieved remarkable things, and those victories deserve celebration. But look at yourself now. Do you keep recounting those past triumphs a little too much?

Do you find yourself narrating old victories to your friends or colleagues? How you used to write thousands of lines of code when you were young; how you used to run several kilometers at a stretch; how you used to wake up early; how you drove a critical project; how you had once climbed a mountain in record time; how you were once fit… If you find yourself narrating the past more than the present, it's a clear sign to reignite the dormant spark. It's time to acknowledge that "your best is yet to come".

The good thing about "best" is that it is a relative term; the only condition being you must be open to acknowledge that there is always a better version. Thus, your best is not just a trophy that is caged in a showcase. It's a vibrant, ever-evolving potential waiting to be refined with every revision, unless you choose to put a mental barrier by declaring your previous best as "the best".

Here are a few strategies to look back at your moments of peak performance you hold dear and move on to surpass those:

- List down your achievements from the past which you consider among your greatest ones.

- Analyze them with a curious and critical mind.

- Ask yourself if there is a better way you could have approached the challenge.

- What new tools, techniques, strategies, or models can make those even better?

- You might have worked out some workaround the last time that's hidden under the carpet. Can you find a better solution?

Remember that you have infinite capacity and limitless potential. Let go of the past, come to terms with the present, and set your sight on the future to make it even more remarkable. Just keep telling yourself, you've done good in the past, but your best is yet to come!

49

Pour in your head, heart and soul

I've written about being passionate several times in this book. Passion is the driving force behind extraordinary achievements. But it's not just passion that's important. Passion must be complimented by intelligence, skill, and humility. Combine these elements and you have a formidable execution strategy that's unshakeable.

Passion explains the "why" behind your actions, igniting the desire to achieve. The intensity of this desire is determined by the depth of your passion, which in turn dictates the urgency with which you pursue your goals. Acknowledging that time is limited creates a sense of urgency, or starvation for time. This starvation stimulates innovative ideas, driving you to accelerate your efforts with intelligent and skillful execution. Once you scale a peak, while you celebrate the victory, it's important to recognize that there's more to be conquered. By remaining undeterred in defeat and humble in victory, you keep the doors open for further learning and progress.

Passion without action is like a beautifully thought story that remains in your heart. Expressing that which resides in your heart requires translating the story in your mind into tangible results, which in turn demands smart application of skills, tools, techniques, and high spirit of mind and body. Remember the countless techniques that you've read throughout this book? Observe yourself, your actions, and your time to help yourself navigate the twists and turns without wasting precious time. This combination of heart and head is oblivious of any domain. Apply it for driving an intricate project, pursuing a hobby, or to simply tweak a routine. It just works! Continuously honing and applying your new-found skills empowers you to bring your vision to life with precision and finesse.

Success can be intoxicating when you achieve your passion backed by your skills and techniques. However, you are perceived to be what you are in entirety, and not just for a goal that you have achieved. That is what humility is all about. People see your dedication, appreciate your expertise, but admire you for the grace with which you handle success. Hon'ble Dr. A P J Abdul Kalam, the former President of India, also known as the Missile Man of India, is a great example on the best use of head, heart, and soul. Despite all his momentous achievements, he remained a curious learner, and humble to be approachable forever. That's a lesson on what makes great personalities so great!

Peak performance isn't just about achieving results; it's about the journey itself and the integrated way to achieve those results. It's about pouring your heart, head, and soul into every step you take. It's about realizing that the process of creation is just as important as the outcome. Thus, liven your passion, sharpen your skills, adopt intelligent execution, and hold on to humility. With this potent combination, you'll be well on your way to creating something truly remarkable.

"Remain grounded to stay all-rounded"

50

Sleep peacefully

Suppose you are working on a demanding project and that's going to span a few months. The project is full of challenges and requires you to be at your energetic best every single day. While each day brings along unprecedented challenges that drain you mentally and physically, the question remains, how do you recharge yourself the next day? It's simple. All you need is a good sleep.

You began your day with great vigor, tackled all the challenges head-on, and achieved all that you wanted to. Yet, come nightfall, and you find yourself struggling to sleep, turning sides, trying to burn down recurring thoughts. Does this sound familiar? Do you find yourself eluded by that peaceful sleep? You're not alone. This experience is ubiquitous, and why not? There's so much stirring of thoughts throughout the day. Your mind finds itself tangled in a web of thoughts.

The result of this sleep deprival is seen in your mental as well as physical energy levels. Sleep deprivation can lead to decreased alertness, impaired decision-making, and reduced immunity levels. Do you think you can pull on for long with this state of your mind and physique? Practically, you can't. All this can adversely affect your performance. So, all you need is a good night's sleep.

Although hectic days are inevitable, at the same time, a peaceful sleep is non-negotiable. Howsoever taxing your day might have been, you must focus on prioritizing your sleep. If you find yourself deprived of deep sleep, here are some techniques to help you switch off and immerse yourself in the darkness of the night.

- ✔ Practice compartmentalization. It's all a mind game. Read the chapter "Learn the art of compartmentalizing" for ideas on how to process emotions in different zones. When you segregate emotions in compartments, you are automatically relieved from the additional activity of stabilizing your mind by untying the mesh of mixed-up thoughts. The freer your mind is, the better will be the quality of your sleep.

✔ Silence the noise of negativity. You may have experienced plenty of unpleasant events during the day. You may have been engaged in disturbing arguments. Burn down all this negativity before going to bed. Avoid dwelling on negativity experienced throughout the day. Go to bed by picturing a refreshing day tomorrow.

✔ Listen to your favorite soundtrack. Music is known to have amazing healing powers. Listening to calm music before bed can help your mind relax. Immersing yourself in music can help stabilize your mind and get a peaceful sleep.

Prioritizing sleep is not weakness, but it is a sign of strength. The above are some simple strategies that you can begin with. Devise your own techniques towards building the ability to fall asleep peacefully and wake up feeling refreshed to conquer anything that comes your way.

"You are the master of your feelings; no one can hurt them without your permission."

Thank you!

When you find yourself on this page, there are two possible scenarios that I consider.
Firstly, perhaps you've just picked up this book for the first time and are flipping through its pages with a quick glance. This is perfectly fine and completely understandable.

On the other hand, you might have delved deeper into the chapters, taking the time to relate them to your own experiences. You might have even decided to implement at least one technique discussed within these pages. If so, I want to express my sincere gratitude to you for being such a patient and engaged reader.

Regardless of which scenario resonates with you, this book consists of the following affirmations and actionable techniques, and I encourage you to persist with your decision with the help of these affirmations.

Thank you for your time and attention! Feel free to reach out to me with your feedback on abhijitkolas@gmail.com.

I'd be happy to consider it in the next edition!

Strength mental
immerse success
manage performance master
longevity strong learn
multitask believe objective comfort
focus thought persist
excel technology
compartment technique
determination
surprise mind art perseverance
sleep leader surprise new
disrupt health creativity
conscious expectation
peak skill perfection
achieve commitment positive
interesting experiment
solution logical emotion
perfect template

www.ingramcontent.com/pod-product-compliance
Lightning Source LLC
LaVergne TN
LVHW061612070526
838199LV00078B/7252